Equality, Rights and the Autonomous Self

*To my brothers, Elmer and Skip, with
thanks for their love and support*

Equality, Rights and the Autonomous Self

Toward a Conservative Economics

Timothy P. Roth, Ph.D.
The University of Texas at El Paso, USA

Edward Elgar
Cheltenham, UK • Northampton, MA, USA

Published by
Edward Elgar Publishing Limited
Glensanda House
Montpellier Parade
Cheltenham
Glos GL50 1UA
UK

Edward Elgar Publishing, Inc.
136 West Street
Suite 202
Northampton
Massachusetts 01060
USA

A catalogue record for this book
is available from the British Library

ISBN 1 84376 450 4

Printed and bound in Great Britain by MPG Books Ltd, Bodmin, Cornwall

Contents

1. The First-Person Self: The Liberal's View

1.1 WHY *THIS* BOOK?

As an economist trained in 'positive', intendedly value-free and institutionless neoclassical economic theory I was, for many years, suspicious of the work of John Rawls. This attitude was informed, in part, by my acquired propensity to question the import into economic analysis of any explicitly normative construals. But it was also animated by what I now appreciate to have been a fundamental misunderstanding of the Kantian/Rawlsian contractarian project. Indeed, in books published in 1999 and 2002 I argue that the Rawlsian institutional imperatives - themselves derivative of a Kantian prior ethical commitment to the moral equivalence of persons - can be deployed both to challenge the economist's consequentialist approach to public policy appraisal, and to provide a rationale for *minimalist* government. The latter is, in turn, a corollary of the indeterminacy of the fundamental theorems of social welfare theory - the economist's theory of the state - and of the imperative to treat all persons impartially.

That I should have arrived at such a conception is surprising, given my intellectual inheritance. It is, after all, commonplace among economists trained in neoclassical doctrine to suppose that their consequentialist theory *is* a theory of minimal government. In fact, it is not. Simply stated, the received instruments of public policy appraisal - the first and second fundamental welfare theorems - have been deployed to rationalize what, I insist, are *ad hoc* government market interventions and income redistribution policies and programs.

Yet, if my account of the limitations of the received doctrine is surprising to many economists, the same might be said of my embrace of Kantian/Rawlsian ethics. On the one hand, economists trained in 'scientific', positive economics regard it - incorrectly - as value-free. For these economists, moral argument and appraisal is 'someone else's business'. On the other hand, their understanding of the Kantian/Rawlsian

1

equality of persons construal suggests to them - as once it did to me - an imperative to promote arbitrary redistribution schemes.[1] My argument - that the moral equivalence of persons has as its corollary minimalist government - will, for many economists, appear to be counterintuitive.

If the Kantian/Rawlsian equality construal is anathema to unreconstructed neoclassical economists, it is integral to what has been characterized as 'high-minded' liberalism. In what follows I shall argue that this project - articulated most effectively in the work of Ronald Dworkin (1985) - employs a conception of equal treatment which contemplates a peculiar and inappropriate understanding of Kantian/Rawlsian equality. Reduced to its essentials, high-minded liberalism demands both that government be neutral with respect to individual perceptions of the 'good life', and that rights be construed as trumps against the intrusion of others' moralistic and other 'external preferences'. In this account, the moral equivalence of persons has as its corollary a tolerance imperative: The agency, independence and dignity of the autonomous self must be respected. In effect, high-minded liberalism regards social norms - or external preferences - as, at minimum, intrusive and, in the limit, as unacceptable.

This construction contrasts sharply with the conservative attitude; a system of beliefs which insists that what 'leads people to see the world in terms of value, and so to develop the transcendental perspective which the liberal requires' is the 'web of attachments' into which a person is born (Scruton 2002, p. 192). In this view, the self is neither transcendental nor autonomous. Immersed in contingent circumstance, agents are both motivated and constrained by the informal and formal institutions, customs and local attachments which, *inter alia,* cultivate the Moral Law. A corollary is that rights are not regarded as trumps against external preferences. Indeed, whereas high-minded liberalism seeks to extend the 'sphere of choice into those realms where traditionally people have sought not permission but constraint' (p. 74), the conservative regards law as legitimately intrusive into 'any area of social life which is vital either to the strength of the social bond, or to the social image of its participants' (p. 73).

In this and subsequent chapters I argue that high-minded liberalism misconstrues Kantian/Rawlsian equality, is internally inconsistent and, given its utilitarian connection, cannot accommodate the moral force of rights. Morever, because it regards utilitarian social welfare theory as instrumental to the achievement of its constitutive political position, high-minded liberalism is encumbered by logical, empirical and ontological problems. In contrast, conservatism is predicated on a conception of the moral agent which is both reconcilable with Kantian/Rawlsian impartiality, and accommodative of what I take to be one of the defining features of observable reality; namely, the path-dependent nature of agents' preference and value structures.

It is perhaps clear that my intellectual commitment to the Kantian/Rawlsian enterprise might, at this cross-section of time, have led me to explore any one of an array of research avenues. Granting this, the motivation for this project may be traced to Professor James Buchanan's catalytic observation, that

> I am sure, from reading this text that you share with me the frustration and irritation of some of our right-wing friends' attitudes toward the whole Rawlsian enterprise, as well as our left-wing adversaries' efforts to co-opt Rawls into their welfarist camp. Admittedly, however, Rawls lends himself to much misinterpretations.

It is both interesting and instructive that the passage is drawn from a letter in which Professor Buchanan reacts to a manuscript which, some months later, emerged as *The Ethics and the Economics of Minimalist Government* (Roth 2002). It is, in any case, Professor Buchanan's imputation of shared 'frustration and irritation' which inspires this work.

In the following pages I seek, first, to show that the Kantian/Rawlsian framework has been misconstrued and misapplied: Whereas high-minded liberalism's constitutive and derivative political positions cannot be reconciled with Kantian/Rawlsian ethics, the same cannot be said of conservatism. Properly understood, conservatism is procedural rather than outcomes-based; it is accommodative of the moral force of rights and, equally important, it deploys a conception of the self which recognizes - as did Kant - that the moral agent's decision environment is shaped, in part, by contingent, empirical conditions.[2] Second, I wish to show that, to embrace the Kanatian/Rawlsian perspective *is* to embrace the conservative point of view. Finally in Chapters 7 and 8 I proffer a view of a conservative economics, and of a conservative theory of law.

1.2 HIGH-MINDED LIBERALISM: AN OVERVIEW

I take as my points of departure the following ideas: (1) That 'the whole Lockean apparatus of natural rights and social contract ... has generally underlain the more high-minded sort of liberalism' (Quinton 1995, p. 250), and (2) That liberalism of this sort 'could fairly be described as the official ideology of the Western world' (Scruton 2002, p. 182). If it is granted that the second statement is not an exercise in hyperbole - and I believe it is not - it follows that interest may legitimately center on Ronald Dworkin's (1985) characterization of high-minded liberalism's constitutive and derivative political positions. In his account, the former are positions 'valued for their own sake', while the latter are regarded as instrumental to the achievement of the constitutive position.

In this and subsequent chapters I shall argue that the particular construals which animate high-minded liberalism's constitutive political position - equality, natural rights and the autonomous self - are logically and empirically flawed. Particular emphasis is placed on the notion upon which the equality and natural rights construals rely: The autonomous self - clearly derivative of Kantian/Rawlsian moral philosophy - is understood to be a transcendental or 'first-person' self.[3] Characteristically, the autonomous self, possessed of free will and reason - and freed of contingent circumstance by a veil of ignorance - is motivated by the Categorical Imperative or Moral Law. In effect, the moral equivalence of persons demands that persons treat each other as ends rather than as means. The institutional imperatives to which this construal gives rise are well known. First, because rights are given lexical priority, the greatest possible equal political participation must be promoted. Second, government must treat each person impartially or 'equally' (Rawls 1971, pp. 221-2).

Because these institutional imperatives are formal rather than substantive they specify neither which rights (duties) are to be respected, nor what, precisely, equal treatment means. A recurring theme of the book is that, in the high-minded liberal's account, the lexical priority of rights contemplates natural rights as trumps against external preferences; against, in other words, agents' preferences with respect to others' consumption or behavior patterns (Dworkin 1985, pp. 196-7). The associated contingent defense of majoritarian democracy is derivative of this understanding of rights: Given the prospect of the tyranny of a majority possessed of external preferences, the minority must be protected against others' equal - but, therefore, contestable - moral tastes or values. For its part, high-minded liberalism's conception of equal treatment by government is not congruent with Kantian/Rawlsian impartiality. Rather, Kantian autonomy - 'the property of the will to be a law to itself' (Kant [1785], 1988 p. 65)[4] - is interpreted to mean that government must treat citizens equally, but that it be 'neutral on what might be called the question of the good life' (Dworkin

1985, p. 191). Thus, if the lexical priority of rights demands that citizens be protected against others' moral (and other) tastes and values, equality of treatment demands that government be neutral on questions of 'the right'; of what the autonomous self ought or ought not do. It is characteristic of high-minded liberalism's constitutive political position, therefore, that government must respect the moral pluralism to which autonomy gives rise while, at the same time, institutionalizing rights designed to protect citizens against the intervention of others' external, including moral, preferences.

1.3   THE CONSTITUTIVE POSITION AND ITS ANTECEDENTS

Interest to this point has centered on an adumbration of what I have characterized as high-minded liberalism's constitutive political position. One might plausibly ask, however, 'are we dealing with liberalism or with liberalisms?' (Ryan 1995, p. 291). It has, after all, become commonplace to distinguish two kinds of liberalism. I refer, of course, to 'classical' and 'modern' liberalism. Because much has been written about both and, in particular, about how they differ, my interest centers on a different question: Is there a sense in which either or both enterprises can be regarded as precursors of high-minded liberalism? Equally important, what is the classical and modern liberal view of equality?

The inquiry may usefully begin with John Locke and Adam Smith, both commonly associated with classical liberalism. As Richard Ashcraft has emphasized.

> A 'right' understanding of the nature and origins of political power, Locke argues, can only be built upon the assumption that all men have 'a perfect Freedom to order their Actions; and dispose of their Possessions, and Persons as they think fit, within the bounds of the Law of Nature, without ... depending upon the Will of any other Man. Since no one has more 'Power' or 'Jurisdiction' than another, this is a 'State also of Equality'. (1994, p. 239)[5]

The passage is heuristic, both because it underscores Locke's propensity to invoke natural rights, and because it emphasizes the Lockean view of the moral equivalence of persons. While nothing in the passage suggests that Locke's views are congruent with the notion that government must be neutral on the question of the good life or the right, it is appropriate again to emphasize that 'the whole Lockean apparatus of natural rights and a social contract ... has generally underlain the more high-minded sort of liberalism' (Quinton 1995, p. 250).[6]

At least in one account, one of the unintended consequences of Adam Smith's 'natural liberty' construal is that it 'would later be taken as a warrant for the notion that "doing what comes naturally" would result in providential outcomes' (Muller 1993, p. 187). Indeed, considered *in vacuo*, the following passage might easily be misinterpreted:

> All systems either of preference or restraint, therefore, being thus completely taken away, the obvious and simple system of natural liberty establishes itself of its own accord. Every man, as long as he does not violate the laws of justice, is left perfectly free to pursue his own interest his own way . (Smith [1776] 1976, p. 687)

As always, however, the passage should not be considered *in vacuo*. The immediately preceding paragraph summarizes Smith's argument against preferential, interventionist policies designed to promote manufacturing, foreign trade or agricultural 'species of industry':

> It is thus that every system which endeavors, either, by extraordinary encouragements, to draw towards a particular species of industry a greater share of the capital of the society than would naturally go to it; or, by extraordinary restraints, to force from a particular species of industry some ... share of the capital which would otherwise be employed in it; is in reality subversive of the great purpose which it means to promote. It retards, instead of accelerating, the progress of the society towards real wealth and greatness; and diminishes, instead of increasing, the real value of the annual produce of its land and labour. (p. 687)

The 'systems either of preference or restraint' to which Smith objected were, in short, mercantilist policies - not the 'despotism of custom' to which John Stuart Mill later referred ([1859] 2000, p. 70). Granting this, one of the unanticipated consequences of Smith's natural liberty construal is that

> The need for institutions to direct the passions, the role of social science in designing institutions, the obligation of government to combat the dangers inherent in commercial society - all would be overlooked. Thus Smith's rhetoric of 'natural liberty' had the paradoxical effect of making his message appear both more conservative and more libertarian than he intended to be. (Muller 1993, p. 187)

The essential point is that, whereas Adam Smith is, as I have emphasized, commonly associated with classical liberalism, his natural liberty conception is not a precursor of high-minded liberalism's constitutive natural rights construal. Whereas the latter imagines a system of natural rights as trumps against external moral and other preferences, Smith emphasized the 'Influence of Custom and Fashion upon Moral Sentiments' ([1759] 1976, pp. 200-211). Indeed, Smith's 'civilizing project' reflected the value he placed in 'the market, the family, and other social institutions for their role in creating that imperfect but attainable level of virtue which he called "decency"' (Muller 1993, p. 188). Central to Smith's civilizing project is the idea that 'to be virtuous is to make our conduct conform to an external model which we have internalized' (Muller 1993, p. 189). And central to this construal is the 'impartial spectator':

> The love and admiration which we naturally conceive for those whose character and conduct we approve of, necessarily dispose us to desire to become ourselves the objects of the like agreeable sentiments ... We must at least believe ourselves to be admirable for what they are admirable. But, in order to attain this satisfaction, we must become the impartial spectators of our own character and conduct ... When seen in this light, if they appear to us as we wish, we are happy and contented. But it greatly confirms this happiness and contentment when we find that other people, viewing them with those very eyes which we, in imagination only, were endeavoring to view them, see them precisely in the same light in which we ourselves had seen them. Their approbation necessarily confirms our own self-approbation. (Smith [1759] 1976, p. 114)

Clearly, the impartial spectator, influenced as he is by family, by tradition, by custom and other 'external' factors is not congruent with the transcendental, autonomous self of high-minded liberalism. Indeed, there is a sense in which Smith's civilizing project is a harbinger of the contemporary conservative philosopher Roger Scruton's account of 'ordinary conscience'. While the nature and implications of ordinary conscience will be more fully adumbrated in Chapter 5, the essence of Scruton's construal is that ordinary conscience, which is born of a 'web of attachments', consists in the strictures of the Kantian Moral Law, the ethic of virtue, sympathy and piety (1996, pp. 120 and 126). In effect,

> The moral being is not merely the [Kantian] rule-governed person who plays the game of rights and duties; he has a distinctive emotional character, which both fits him for the moral life and extends and modifies its edicts. He is a creature of extended sympathies, motivated by love, admiration, shame and a host of other social emotions. (Scruton 1996, pp. 113-14)

It seems clear that this account of what could be characterized as the endogenous and exogenous (or social) sources of moral reasoning and appraisal is broadly congruent with Smith's civilizing project. Indeed, it seems plausible to conclude that Scruton's 'impartial judge' (1996, p. 120) is at least vaguely reminiscent of Smith's impartial spectator.[7] Equally significant, Scruton's *The Meaning of Conservatism* (2002) emphasizes the limitations of high-minded liberalism's conception of the transcendental autonomous self. Roughly paraphrased, the Kantian, transcendental first-person self has no motive to act; agency requires immersion in the '"empirical conditions" of the human agent' (p. 189). That these and other ideas are central to what Scruton characterizes as a 'conservative vision' (p. 192) is itself of interest. That it finds expression in Smith's *The Theory of Moral Sentiments* is revealing:

> When I endeavour to examine my own conduct. ... I divide myself, as it were, into two persons. ... The first is the spectator. ... The second is the agent, the person whom I properly call myself, and of whose conduct, under the character of a spectator, I was endeavouring to form some opinion. The first is the judge; the second the person judged. (p. 113)

Whether these (and other) considerations may lead one to conclude that Adam Smith 'is a nonliberal thinker' (Khalil 2002, p. 670) is not of immediate interest. What does seem clear is that nothing in Smith's work may be regarded as contributory to high-minded liberalism's natural rights and transcendental, autonomous self construals.

While I shall have more to say in Chapter 7 about the relationship between Smith's work and what I characterize as a conservative economics, I turn now to a consideration of modern liberalism. I take as my point of departure that the latter is 'exemplified by John Stuart Mill's *On Liberty*' (Ryan 1995, p. 294).[8]

If Smith emphasized the role of custom in the formation of conscience, Mill, in the romantic tradition (Muller 1993, pp. 191-3), emphasized individuality and perfectibility:

> The despotism of custom is everywhere the standing hindrance to human advancement, being in unceasing antagonism to that disposition to aim at something better than customary, which is called, according to circumstances, the spirit of liberty, or that of progress and improvement . ... The progressive principle, however, in either shape, whether as the love of liberty or of improvement, is antagonistic to the sway of Custom, involving at least emancipation from that yoke;

and the contest between the two constitutes the chief interest of the history of mankind. ([1859] 2000, p. 70)

Importantly, the 'spirit of liberty' extended, in Mill's account, to morality:

the appropriate region of human liberty ... comprises, first, the inward domain of consciousness; liberty of thought and feeling; absolute freedom of opinion and sentiment on all subjects, practical or speculative, scientific, moral, or theological. ([1859] 2000, p. 15)[9]

It would, however, be inappropriate to conclude that there is a one-to-one correspondence between Mill's moral liberty and the moral pluralism associated with high-minded liberalism. Mill is clear that, whereas the individual is 'not accountable to society' insofar as his actions 'concern the interests of no person but himself', he is also clear that social or legal punishment is appropriate 'if society is of the opinion that the one or the other is requisite for [society's] protection' ([1859] 2000, p. 94). Indeed, Mill is explicit about behavior which 'might be justly punished'. He suggests, *inter alia*, that gambling, drunkenness, incontinence, idleness, uncleanliness (p. 80), intemperance, extravagance (p. 81), and 'bad example set to others by the vicious or the self-indulgent' (p. 83) are cases that may be 'taken out of the province of liberty, and placed in that of morality or law' (p. 82). Moreover, fraud, sanitary precautions, the functions of police, drug labeling, contract provisions, child support, and 'offenses against decency' may all, properly, be regulated by the state (pp. 95-8). Finally, 'the State should require and compel the education, up to a certain standard, of every human being who is born its citizen' (p. 105).

While the list is not exhaustive, it is heuristic. Whatever else is said, Mill 'cherished an ideal of strenuous self-improvement and disinterested moral concern' ([1859] 2000, p. xvii). Relatedly, he regarded society as 'the protector of all its members' (p. 80). It seems appropriate to conclude, then, that Mill's views are irreconcilable with high-minded liberalism's rights as trumps construal. Stated differently, in Mill's world, rights are not properly regarded as trumps against persons' external preferences. His view of the despotism of custom notwithstanding, 'perfect freedom' does not, *inter alia*, extend to externality-generating actions:

> The State, while it respects the liberty of each in what specially regards himself, is
> bound to maintain a vigilant control over his exercise of any power which it allows
> him to possess over others. ([1859] 2000, p. 104)

If Mill's views cannot be regarded as reconcilable with the natural rights
as trumps against external preferences construal, the same is true of his
generic view of natural rights. In fact, 'Mill always remained enough of a
Utilitarian to disdain general talk of rights, certainly of "natural rights"...
But legal rights he considered of fundamental importance' ([1859] 2000,
pp. xx-xxi). Equally important, Mill was critical of Jeremy Bentham, the
father of utilitarianism, because Bentham had no way to account for the role
of conscience. In Mill's account, man is capable

> of desiring for its own sake the conformity of his own character to his standard of
> excellence, without hope of good or fear of evil from other source than his own
> inward consciousness. ([1838] 1990, pp. 97-8)

As we shall see, this formulation is closer to the view of the conservative
philosopher, Scruton, than it is to high-minded liberalism.

1.4   DWORKIN'S 'LIBERALISM'

Granting the logic of what has been said, high-minded liberalism is not
congruent with what has been characterized as classical or modern
liberalism. Yet, as has twice been emphasized, the 'Lockean apparatus of
natural rights and a social contract ... has generally underlain the more
high-minded sort of liberalism';[10] the liberalism whose constitutive political
position has been articulated by Ronald Dworkin (1985, pp. 181-204). On
the one hand, it is tautological that the natural rights as trumps against
external preferences construal is a natural right-based political morality.
On the other hand, Dworkin's conceptions of equality and of the
transcendental, autonomous self are rooted in Kantian/Rawlsian
contractarianism; in the idea of morality as impartiality (Kymlicka 1993,
pp. 191-5). In his account, the moral equivalence of persons demands that
the agency, independence, dignity and autonomy of the individual be
respected. *Inter alia*, Dworkin's autonomous self construal rules out 'the
state's use of coercion to make people morally better' (G. Dworkin 1995,
p. 363). In effect, the authority and legitimacy of the state depends upon
its respect for an 'endorsement constraint':

[Dworkin] develops an argument against state paternalism which ... relies on the idea that the good life for persons is necessarily one that they create for themselves, that is lived from the inside as opposed to led from the outside. He argues for what Kymlicka has called the 'endorsement constraint'. (G. Dworkin 1995, p. 363)

The essential idea is that neither government policy nor statutory, common or constitutional law 'can make a person's life better against his opinion that it does not' (Dworkin 1991, p. 50).[11] Failure to respect this stricture is violative of autonomy, and corrosive of the state's authority and legitimacy.

Given this background, it is appropriate now to develop more fully the character and content of high-minded liberalism. Interest centers, in particular, on an essay which anticipates and answers the question posed by Alan Ryan: 'Is liberalism determinately describable at all. ...' (1995, p. 291). In the essay entitled 'Liberalism' Dworkin proposed 'a theory about what liberalism is' (1985, pp. 181-204). On the presumption that liberalism 'is an authentic and coherent political morality', Dworkin argues that 'a certain conception of equality, which I shall call the liberal conception of equality, is the nerve of liberalism' (p. 183). In his account, any coherent political program consists of two elements: 'constitutive political positions that are valued for their own sake, and derivative positions that are valued as strategies, as means of achieving the constitutive positions' (pp. 183-4).

I shall argue here, and in later chapters, that whereas Dworkin insists that it is not 'constitutive of liberalism' (pp. 201-2), utilitarianism is, in fact, characteristic of liberalism's constitutive and derivative political positions. With this discussion momentarily deferred, I focus on Dworkin's characterization of the two positions.

Dworkin takes as his points of departure that 'there is broad agreement within modern politics that the government must treat all its citizens with equal concern and respect', but that 'Different people hold ... very different conceptions of what that abstract principle requires in particular cases' (p. 191). In effect, Dworkin assumes that modern politics is animated by the Kantian/Rawlsian idea of the moral equivalence of persons.[12] Granting this, the question becomes: 'What does it mean for the government to treat its citizens as equals?' Dworkin suggests that the question may be answered in 'two fundamentally different ways':

The first supposes that government must be neutral on what might be called the question of the good life. The second supposes that government cannot be neutral on that question, because it cannot treat its citizens as equal human beings without a theory of what human beings ought to be. (p. 191)

Whereas Dworkin insists that liberalism 'takes as its constitutive political morality the first conception of morality' (p. 192), he associates the second with conservatism:

> The conservative supposes that the good man would wish to be treated in accordance with the principles of a special sort of society, which I shall call the virtuous society . ... the conservative is distinct in believing that his own society, with its present institutions, is a virtuous society for the special reason that its history and common experience are better guides to sound virtue than any non-historical and therefore abstract deduction of virtue from first principles could provide. (pp. 198-9)

In Chapter 5 I shall argue that Dworkin's characterization of the conservative's constitutive political position is broadly reconcilable with Adam Smith's civilizing project and, to a lesser extent, with Mill's 'disinterested moral concern'. Setting this aside, at least for the moment, the question becomes, What are the institutional imperatives to which high-minded liberalism's [hereafter, 'the liberal's'] definition of equality gives rise?

To answer this question, Dworkin supposes that a liberal is asked to found a new state. The hypothetical liberal is required to 'dictate [the new state's] constitution and fundamental institutions. He must propose a general theory of political distribution, that is, a theory of how whatever the community has to assign, by way of goods or resources or opportunities, should be assigned' (p. 192). Dworkin suggests, quite plausibly, that the liberal 'will arrive initially at something like this principle of rough equality: resources and opportunities should be distributed, so far as possible, equally' (p. 192). Given that 'citizens have different theories of the good and hence different preferences' he concludes that

> The liberal, as lawgiver, ... needs mechanisms to satisfy the principles of equal treatment in spite of these disagreements. He will decide that there are no better mechanisms available, as general political institutions, than the two main institutions of our own political economy: the economic market, for decisions about what goods shall be produced and how they shall be distributed, and representative democracy, for collective decisions about what conduct shall be prohibited or regulated. (pp. 193-4)

Granting all of this, the economic market and representative democracy are among the liberal's key derivative political positions. In this account, both are instrumental to the achievement of the liberal's constitutive political position. Yet, given 'the anti-egalitarian consequences of free enterprise in practice' (p. 194), and given that persons possess 'external preferences ... about what others shall do or have' (p. 196), the liberal will choose a mixed economic system (p. 196), and institutionalize a system of rights against the intervention of external preferences (p. 197).

On the presumption that the market can - presumably, through appropriate government market intervention - 'be made to work efficiently' (p. 194), there is still the problem that the 'liberal lawgiver ... faces a difficult task':

> His conception of equality requires an economic system that produces certain inequalities (those that reflect the true differential costs of goods and opportunities) but not others (those that follow from differences in ability, inheritance, and so on). The market produces both the required and the forbidden inequalities, and there is no alternative system that can be relied upon to produce the former without the latter. (pp. 195-6)

It is significant that, in his adumbration of what could be characterized as the perfectibility of the economic system, Dworkin invokes the first and second fundamental welfare theorems; theorems - derivative of utilitarian social welfare theory - which have been characterized as the economist's theory of the state (Brennan 1995, p. 142). The first fundamental welfare theorem asserts that a perfectly competitive system will automatically move to a first-best Pareto-optimal or 'efficient' outcome. For its part, the second fundamental welfare theorem indicates that, no matter to which 'competitive' equilibrium an economic system is impelled, a 'socially desired' allocation can be realized by appeal to lump-sum taxes and bounties (Roth 2002, p. 34). While discussion of the two theorems and, *pari passu*, of the economist's theory of the state, is deferred to Chapters 4 and 6, it is sufficient for present purposes to note that lump-sum taxes and bounties are, in principle, those which do not affect relative prices (Roth 2002, pp. 54-5). Given this understanding, it is significant that, in light of the propensity of the market to produce 'both the required and the forbidden inequalities',

> The liberal must be tempted, therefore, to a reform of the market through a scheme of redistribution that leaves its pricing system relatively intact but sharply limits,

at least, the inequalities in welfare that his initial principle prohibits. (Dworkin 1985, p. 196)

It is clear, then, that the liberal's derivative political position is inexorably bound up with the economist's theory of the state; with utilitarian social welfare theory.   As we shall see, this 'utilitarian connection' gives rise to fundamental logical, empirical, and ontological problems.

If, in Dworkin's account, the market system is perfectible, the same is true of representative democracy. He suggests, first, that 'Democracy is justified because it enforces the right of each person to respect and concern as an individual'. Yet, 'in practice, the decisions of a democratic majority may often violate that right, according to the liberal theory of what the right requires' (p. 196). Here, the potential tyranny of the majority attaches to the presence of external preferences; of 'preferences people have about what others shall do or have'. By way of illustration, Dworkin suggests the following:

> Suppose a legislature elected by a majority decides to make criminal some act (like speaking in favor of an unpopular political position, or participating in eccentric sexual practices), not because the act deprives others of opportunities they want, but because the majority disapproves of these views or that sexual morality.   The political decision, in other words, reflects ... the domination of one set of external preferences; that is, preferences people have about what others shall do or have. This decision invades rather than enforces the right of citizens to be treated as equals. (p. 196)

The proffered solution finds its genesis in Lockean natural rights; in the idea that the 'equality of Men by Nature' implies that all men have a 'perfect freedom to order their Actions, and dispose of their Possessions, and Persons as they think fit, within the Law of Nature, without ... depending upon the Will of any other Man' (S 1.2).[13] In Dworkin's account,

> The liberal ... needs a scheme of civil rights whose effect will be to determine those political decisions that are antecedently likely to reflect strong external preferences and to remove those decisions from majoritarian political institutions altogether. The scheme of rights necessary to do this will depend on general facts about the prejudices and other external preferences of the majority at any given time, and different liberals will disagree about what is needed at any particular time. (1985, p. 197)

This, in short, is Dworkin's familiar rights as trumps construal.[14] Significantly (for the argument developed in later chapters), Dworkin's 'general theory of rights' may be regarded as an attempt to perfect both majoritarian democracy and utilitarianism:

> The concept of an individual political right, in the strong anti-utilitarian sense I distinguished earlier, is a response to the philosophical defects of a utilitarianism that counts external preferences and the practical impossibility of a utilitarianism that does not. It allows us to enjoy the institutions of political democracy, which enforce overall or unrefined utilitarianism, and yet protect the fundamental right of citizens to equal concern and respect by prohibiting decisions that seem, antecedently, likely to have been reached by virtue of the external components of the preferences democracy reveals. (1978, p. 277)[15]

Once again, high-minded liberalism's utilitarian connection is clear. It follows, *pari passu*, that liberalism of this sort is a hybrid moral theory.[16] Because it assigns an instrumental role to rights (as trumps against external preferences), liberalism incorporates elements of right-based moral theories. And, because it incorporates elements of utilitarian social welfare theory it incorporates elements of goal-based moral theories. Granting this, it seems clear that insufficient attention has centered on the fundamental irreconcilability of right- and goal-based moral theories and, therefore, on the logical opposition between liberalism and utilitarianism. Equally important, insufficient account has been take of the irreconcilability of the Kantian/Rawlsian theory of the right - the moral equivalence of persons - and the utilitarian theory of the good. While these ideas are more fully developed in Chapter 4, I note for the moment Rawls' admonition that 'The fault of the utilitarian doctrine is that it mistakes impersonality for impartiality' (1971, p. 190).

1.5   THE LIBERAL PARADOX

If high-minded liberalism must contend with the irreconcilability of right- and goal-based moral theories, it must also confront the 'contradiction [which] arises from [its] Kantian attempt to justify rights from the first-person perspective' (Scruton 2002, p. 189).

While the contradiction to which I refer is developed more fully in later chapters, the essential point is this:

> the Kantian abstraction invites me to think of myself as the subject of an insoluble dilemma: either I am a transcendental self, obedient to reason, in which case I

cannot act, or else I am able to act, in which case my motives are part of my circumstance and history, and remain unresponsive to the voice of reason, which calls always from beyond the horizon of the empirical world. The supposition that I am a concrete, historical agent of change, and at the same time bound to recognize the rights of others, becomes contradictory. (p. 189)

It is clear that the Kantian/Rawlsian autonomous self - the conception which, *inter alia*, animates the rights as trumps construal - is a transcendental or first-person self. In this account, the self, freed of contingent circumstance, and ensconced behind a veil of ignorance, deploys reason to derive the Kantian Moral Law. While, as Scruton suggests, each of us is 'compelled to think in this way whenever he asks himself not, what shall I do, but what ought I to do' (pp. 190-91), this is not exhaustive of the dimensions of moral argument and appraisal.

While high-minded liberalism deploys the transcendental, autonomous self construal both to explain the value of freedom and to 'define the sphere of privacy within which the individual resides' (p. 184), the transcendental self has no motive to act: 'Clearly, a transcendental self, outside nature and outside the "empirical conditions" of the human agent has no capacity to act here and now' (p. 189). While it is precisely the transcendental self upon whom the liberal relies in deriving - and justifying - his rights as trumps construal, a question remains: Assuming that, behind the veil of ignorance, the transcendental self chooses to treat each person as an end in himself, what is it that binds him to respect the associated rights and correlative duties after the veil has been lifted? The point is precisely that, when the veil is lifted, the agent is immersed in contingent circumstance; in the web of attachments which define his local, transitory and path-dependent social bonds. Under such conditions,

> The only justification that can be found for the virtuous stance that [the first person perspective] recommends to me - the stance of justice, in which I extend to others an active recognition of their rights - is to be found in the long-term benefit conferred upon humanity, by our desire to deal equitably with each other. But this justification is not a first-person reason for action. (p. 190)

In short, once the veil of ignorance is removed, respect for rights and duties - however they are construed - depends upon a third-person perspective. I shall argue that this perspective is informed, not only by the ruminations of the transcendental self situated behind a veil of ignorance but, as well, by the other components of ordinary conscience (Scruton 1996, pp. 120 and 126). While the notion of ordinary conscience will be developed in later chapters, it is sufficient for present purposes to note that

> A security ordered entirely by the moral law, in which rights, duties and justice take precedence over all interests and affections, would alienate the mere human beings who compose it, and soon fall apart. For it would make no distinction between neighbours and strangers, between the alien and the friend. People need the safety promised by the moral law, and by the habit of negotiation. But they also need something more: the nexus of affection and sympathy which binds them to their neighbours, which creates a common destiny, and which leads people to share one another's sorrows and joys. (1996, p. 113)

That this is vaguely reminiscent of Smith's civilizing project is clear. That it finds no counterpart in high-minded liberalism's conception of the autonomous, transcendental self is also clear. Reduced to its essentials, exclusive reliance on the autonomously generated Moral Law precludes an explicit accounting of other, exogenously determined, and path-dependent sources of moral reasoning. While questions of right, duty and responsibility are the province of the Moral Law, the ethic of virtue, sympathy and piety are also instruments of moral argument and appraisal. These, however, are not autonomously generated. They are nurtured, intertemporally, by the interaction of the formal and informal institutions, customs, traditions and local attachments which characterize a society. Together, these four sources of moral reasoning constitute ordinary conscience. Both endogenously and exogenously determined, it is this ordinary conscience which, in part, animates and constrains action. Yet, given its commitment to the moral sovereignty of the transcendental, first-person self, high-minded liberalism denies the legitimacy of moral imperatives borne of contingent, societal impulses. Indeed, it is precisely these exogenously generated behavioral norms which motivate the rights as trumps construal.

1.6   THE TOLERANCE IMPERATIVE

It has been suggested that, 'Whatever liberalism involves, it certainly includes toleration and an antipathy to closing ranks around any system of beliefs' (Ryan 1995, p. 292). In the case of high-minded liberalism, this is a corollary of its insistence that autonomous individuals have the natural right to choose among very different, but equally good lives. The imperative, in short, is to be non-judgmental; 'to leave as much moral and political space around every person as is compatible with the demands of social life' (Scruton 2002, p. 182). It is precisely this concern which animates the liberal's demand that a scheme of civil rights against external preferences be embedded in the constitutional rules of the political game (Dworkin 1985, p. 197). What is perhaps less clear is that the tolerance imperative has broader implications for what Scruton has called the 'legitimate sphere of law' (2002, p. 68). In the liberal's account, this reduces to the view that statutory and common law may properly be regarded as distributors of constitutional rights (p. 73). In anticipation of the argument developed in Chapter 8, it is sufficient to emphasize that this construal contrasts sharply with the conservative view. The latter regards the law as embodying 'the fundamental values of society' (p. 7). In this account, respect for prevailing social values is both a *sine qua non* for the authority of the law, and justificatory of law's intrusion into 'any area of social life which is vital either to the strength of the social bond, or to the social image of its participants' (p. 73).

If the tolerance imperative has implications for constitutional, statutory and common law, the same might be said of other, formal institutions. The dominance of the educational establishment's 'psychological strategy' is of particular interest (Chapter 2).

Finally, the potential conflict between (apparently) intrinsically valuable tolerance on the one hand, and intolerance of external preferences on the other, is explored in later chapters. For the moment, I emphasize that

> The tolerance that autonomy-based liberalism justifies may ... turn out to be narrow in scope. Susan Mendus argues that autonomy-based liberalism justifies toleration only toward 'those diverse forms of life which themselves value autonomy and thus makes toleration a pragmatic device'. (Macedo 1995, p. 624)

1.7   PLAN OF THE BOOK

While Chapter 1 has concentrated on high-minded liberalism's constitutive political position, Chapter 2 focuses on liberalism's derivative political positions.

Given liberalism's conception of the Kantian Moral Law, the moral equivalence of persons demands that the transcendental first-person self be sovereign; that morality be subjectively determined. Granting this, society's formal and informal institutions must serve 'as means to the end of individual freedom' and promote 'equality' (Scruton 2002, p. 38). While the associated institutional imperatives take many forms, particular interest centers on education policy. The symbiosis between liberalism's constitutive moral pluralism and the ethical neutrality of secular psychology accounts, I argue, for the dominance of the educational establishment's 'psychological strategy'. Here, the 'moral individual envisioned is one who somehow transcends time, space, relationships, and culture ... but serves some thin notions of the common good when he or she freely chooses' (Hunter 2000, p. 11). While much of the discussion in Chapter 2 centers on this psychological strategy, the balance of the chapter focuses on liberalism's diversity imperative, and on a preliminary discussion of liberalism's social justice construal.

Chapter 3 centers on a critical appraisal of the liberal's conception of equal treatment, and of the related natural rights and social justice construals. I argue, *inter alia*, that the notion that the government ought to be neutral on the question of the good life - of what the 'good person' ought or ought not do - is, itself, a theory of the good. I argue, moreover, that the liberal's transcendental, first-person perspective is both irreconcilable with Kantian/Rawlsian ethics, and non-accommodative of the dimensions of moral discussion and appraisal which recognize 'the unquestionable rightness of local, transitory and historically conditioned social bonds' (Scruton 2002, p. 192). Following Scruton, I argue that the liberal's institutional skepticism - the propensity always to ask, 'Why should I do that' - is corrosive of the 'natural piety' borne of these attachments. Granting this, the relentless questioning of society's informal and formal institutions - itself a corollary of the moral pluralism associated with self-generated morality - erodes the conditions which nurture the true, Kantian first-person perspective.

As was suggested in Chapter 1, the fundamental problem is that the Kantian first-person perspective - the impartiality of the veil of ignorance constrained transcendental self - cannot generate a motive for action. For this, the agent must invoke his 'empirical self'; a self subject to the contingencies of desire, extant circumstance, and historically-driven path-dependencies. It is these empirical conditions which motivate the question of agency, of action. Given a motive to act, Kantian rights and duties - the imperative of the Moral Law - must, insofar as it is feasible, be respected. When, however, the Moral Law 'neither forbids nor permits an action, there is still the question whether a virtuous person would perform it' (Scruton 1996, p. 125); whether, in other words, the ethic of virtue, sympathy and piety - the respect for law, civil order and other sacred things - would permit it. It is precisely because these exogenously generated 'traditional virtues' endorse, supplement and nurture the Moral Law that they should be cultivated. Instead, the institutional skepticism of the morally sovereign autonomous first-person self 'corrode(s) the conditions which nurture it' (Scruton 2002, p. 193).

If, as we have seen, the liberal is skeptical of formal and informal institutions, he rejects *a priori* the role of external preferences; preferences against which he asserts the 'the right of citizens to be treated as equals' (Dworkin 1985, p. 196). Significantly, the liberal acknowledges that such preferences may be political, altruistic or moralistic. Granting this, a central focus of Chapter 3 is a critical appraisal of the entire natural rights enterprise, and of the liberal's particular natural rights construal.

While the existence of natural rights might properly be characterized as an unsettled philosophical question, natural justice is understood to be a procedural notion. As such, 'it has no application to states of affairs, as such, judged independently of the agency which produced it' (pp. 79-80). Set against this is the liberal's 'social justice' construal. The balance of Chapter 3 is given over to an adumbration of the 'deep and inevitable conflict' between natural and social justice (p. 86).

Chapter 4 focuses on the liberal's utilitarian connection. I emphasize, first, that consequentialism in any form is irreconcilable with liberalism's Kantian roots. That said, it is clear that the liberal deploys utilitarianism - the theory of the good which is most standardly employed to fill out the consequentialist framework - both in his constitutive and in his derivative political positions. In the first instance, the justificatory argument for his natural rights construal relies on external preferences; on interpersonal effects in agents' utility functions. It is tautological that this is a utilitarian conception. Moreover, the liberal endorses utilitarianism because 'Utilitarian arguments of policy ... embody the fundamental right of equal concern and respect, because they treat the wishes of each member of the community on a par with the wishes of any other' (Dworkin 1978, p. 275). In this respect, it is clear that the liberal both mistakes utilitarian impersonality for impartiality (Rawls 1971, p. 190), and fails to take account of the fact that utilitarianism cannot accommodate the moral force of rights. Granting this, I argue that the liberal's constitutive political morality is internally inconsistent: Because 'evaluation of conduct from a utilitarian standpoint is dominated by direct utilitarian arguments and therefore ignores the moral force of justified legal rights' (Lyons 1982, p. 113), the liberal cannot deploy utilitarian logic to justify the rights he seeks to protect.

If the liberal's utilitarian connection is irreconcilable with his constitutive political morality, the view that utilitarian social welfare theory is instrumental to the achievement of his constitutive position raises fundamental logical, empirical and ontological issues.

I emphasize, again, that consequentialist morality cannot be reconciled with the Kantian first-person perspective. Despite this, it is clear, as we saw in Chapter 1, that the liberal regards the economist's theory of the state, social welfare theory, as instrumental to the achievement of 'good ends'. It is part of the liberal's derivative political project to deploy the theory's first and second fundamental welfare theorems - the first to justify government market interventions, the second to justify income redistribution. Given the logical, empirical and ontological problems which attend it, I argue that policies informed by social welfare theory must be regarded as *ad hoc*. Emphasis is placed on the indeterminacy of both the efficiency or welfare frontier and the social welfare function. I show, moreover, that even it if were determinate, the path to the frontier is not assured. The fundamental problem is that the moral force of rights cannot, on utilitarian terms, be respected.

Chapter 5 develops the conservative's constitutive political position. Emphasis is placed on what has been characterized as the 'paradox of liberalism' (S 1.5). As the analysis deployed in Chapter 1 suggests, in his single-minded pursuit of freedom, the liberal endorses a subjective, first-person morality. While his enterprise is grounded in the Kantian idea of an autonomous, transcendental self, unencumbered by contingent circumstance, the liberal takes no account of the fact that it is contingent, empirical conditions - including formal and informal institutions - which animate and constrain action. In effect, if the self were transcendental - constrained, as it were, by a veil of ignorance - it could not act. Granting this, the first-person perspective must be supplemented by what Scruton has called the third-person point of view; a perspective 'in which people are seen to be immersed in the contingencies of social life, acting from passions which respond to the changing circumstances of existence' (2002, p. 190).

In this account, the vision of the good is not a subjectively determined ought. Rather, it is the 'concrete, immediate "ought" of family' and other social bonds (p. 192). And it is precisely this socially cultivated empirical ought 'that leads people to see the world in terms of value, and so to develop the transcendental perspective which the liberal requires' (p. 192). In effect, the transcendental first-person perspective cannot, as Kant acknowledged, be sustained. It can, however, be cultivated. But this, in turn, requires that the other dimensions of moral argument and appraisal -

the ethic of virtue, sympathy and piety or respect for formal institutions - not be the subject of relentless institutional skepticism and the associated 'reforming spirit'.

While the practice of ordinary conscience - the interplay of the four sources of moral reasoning (Chapter 1) - is briefly revisited, the focus of Chapter 5 is the implications of this construal for the broader, conservative constitutive political position. Central to this project is a rejection of the liberal view of law as a distributor of natural rights. In the conservative view, rights are not properly regarded as trumps against external preferences. Insofar as these interpersonal effects subsume political, altruistic and moralistic preferences or values - each of which is shaped, in part, by social attachments - 'any area of social life which is vital to the strength of the social bond, or to the social image of its participants, will be one into which the law may legitimately intrude' (Scruton 2002, p. 73). *Inter alia*, this 'collusion between social values and legal norms' (p. 132) is antithetical to the moral pluralism to which the liberal's first-person perspective gives rise. Equally important, it is consonant with Kant's view that all political issues - including the character and content of legal rights - are moral issues (Kersting 1992, p. 343). The implications for statutory and common law, as well as for the constitution which constrains both, are adumbrated in Chapter 5, and are more fully explored in Chapter 8.

If the conservative rejects the rights as trumps construal, he also contests the liberal's conception of equality. Given that morality is not the exclusive province of the autonomous, first-person self, perceptions of the good life can neither be subjectively determined nor immune from societal scrutiny. Granting this, the imperative of government policy is not tolerance (Chapter 1). Rather, it is that government must treat persons impartially - subject to the constraints imposed by a constitution informed neither by natural rights nor by moral pluralism. Rather, the constitution should, in the Kantian/Rawlsian sense, maximize equal political participation. It is in this way that, *inter alia*, perceptions of the good life - of how individuals ought to live - may find political expression. For their part, perceptions of the good life, or moralistic external preferences are, in this account, informed not by the liberal's transcendental first-person self, but by the four sources of moral argument; by the Kantian Moral Law, by virtue, by sympathy and by piety.

If the conservative seeks, by constitutional and other means, to give voice to external preferences, he is concerned with the rent seeking which characterizes representative, majoritarian democracy. While the nature of, and catalysts to, rent seeking are explicated in Chapter 6, the essential point is that special interest rent seeking is intendedly discriminatory. Given that post-constitutional conflictual politics is congenial to such opportunistic behavior - a concern of America's founders - a case can be made for appropriate constitutional constraints.

Finally, whereas the liberal regards utilitarian social welfare theory - the economist's theory of the state - as instrumental to the achievement of social ends, the theory finds no place in the conservative's constitutive or derivative political positions. On the one hand, while the theory's fundamental constructs - the efficiency frontier and the social welfare function - are indeterminate, the first and second fundamental welfare theorems are deployed to justify both government market interventions and income redistribution schemes (Chapter 4). In effect, the theory has facilitated the discriminatory rent seeking which the conservative abhors. On the other hand, the theory can accommodate neither the moral force of rights, nor any plausible theory of justice. Finally, because it is consequentialist, its focus, in liberal hands, is the promotion of social justice - an ephemeral concept for which no settled definition exists (Chapter 3).

Chapter 6 concentrates on an adumbration of some conservative derivative political positions. Given the symbiotic relationship between the liberal's constitutive moral pluralism and the ethical neutrality of the educational establishment's psychological strategy (Chapter 2), particular interest centers on the latter. If the liberal's autonomous, transcendental self determines morality for himself, secular psychology's working assumption is that 'character resides within each of us, largely independent of the relationships we have or the communities into which we are born. These endowments only need to be coaxed out and developed within the personality' (Hunter 2000, p. 10). I argue, *inter alia*, that this moral pedagogy ignores the exogenous, culturally determined sources of ordinary conscience (Chapter 5). Simply stated, the ethic of virtue, sympathy and piety are not endogenously determined. They are reinforced by habits institutionalized within a moral community (p. 19). To deny their role in the formation of ordinary conscience is, implicitly, to erode the constraints that make both civil society and freedom possible.

Equally important, the liberal's tolerance imperative has an analogue in psychological moral pedagogy. While the liberal says that one must give moral and political space to the autonomous, self-determining self (Chapter 1), 'the enduring subtext in the evolution of moral education in America ... has been the quest for inclusiveness' (p. 205). Understood to mean the unquestioning acceptance of disparate, subjectively determined moral judgments, it is clear that inclusiveness underwrites the liberal's institutional skepticism project: The moral authority of culturally determined behavioral norms must be justified to the autonomous, transcendental self. The implications of this moral freedom imperative are explored in Chapter 6. I emphasize, *inter alia*, the Madisonian idea that common moral ideals are the 'parchment barriers' that protect individual liberties (Krause 2002, p.ix). Granting this, these ideals are too important to be left to the caprice of 'self-realization', 'self-actualization', or 'diversity'.

The balance of Chapter 6 is motivated by the idea, developed in Chapter 5, that all political issues are moral issues. That said, given the logical, empirical and ontological problems associated with the economist's theory of the state (Chapter 4), the desideratum is not consequentialist. The conservative's derivative political positions are animated neither by invocations of the first or second fundamental welfare theorems nor by ill-defined notions of social justice or progress. Rather, the imperative is procedural.

I stipulate first that agents' decision environments are characterized by bounded rationality, information asymmetry and, *pari passu*, opportunistic behavior. It follows that high *ex ante* and *ex post* transaction or monitoring costs are endemic to post-constitutional, conflictual politics. The decision environment is therefore congenial to 'logrolling', to rent seeking, and to majoritarian cycling - each of which is fundamentally discriminatory. Granting this, omnibus or 'bundling' legislation must be constitutionally prohibited, and government on-, off- and off-off-budget activity must be subject to a constitutional impartiality or generality constraint.

Emphasis is placed on the difference between the impartiality envisioned here, and the liberal's conception of equality. The latter stipulates that government must treat autonomous, first-person selves equally, while remaining neutral on what might be called the question of the good life (Chapter 1). The liberal may, therefore, imagine an *a priori* constitutional constraint which instructs legislators to disregard the external preferences of their constituents (Dworkin 1985, p. 197). The constitutional impartiality constraint envisioned here contemplates no such prohibition. Rather, voters' external preferences - their political, altruistic and moralistic values - are understood to 'count'. Granting this, whatever policies are endorsed, they must not discriminate among affected parties.

Significantly, such a construal would prohibit both intra- and intergenerational discrimination.

With this in mind, I concentrate on the development of some examples which are, I believe, heuristic. I emphasize, again, that policies informed by the first and second fundamental welfare theorems are ruled out. That said, which policies may be endorsed, given voters' strictly personal *and* external preferences, cannot be determined *a priori*. Indeed, given the endogeneity or path-dependent nature of preference and value structures, policy endorsements may be expected intertemporally to change. Nevertheless, we can say, *a priori*, that certain policy issues must always be faced. Among these are taxation, government spending, credit and redistribution or transfer programs, deficit finance and regulatory policies. The argument suggests that a proportional income or expenditure tax would be consistent with intragenerational impartiality. For its part, the government spending discussion is complicated by the analytical distinction between pure public and excludable or private goods. Given the indeterminacy of the first-best Pareto optimal outcome and the imperative to eliminate discriminatory rent seeking, I argue that government provision of public goods should contemplate a proportional tax rate defined on a broad tax base. Moreover, whether employed in the production of public or excludable goods, government input demand must be impartially distributed. Finally, discriminatory subsidization of excludable goods, whatever the desired outcome, must be constitutionally prohibited. Given that they are characterized by in-period and intergenerational discrimination, the same is true of government credit programs.

Other examples contemplate transfer programs, deficit finance and regulatory policies. A recurring theme is that each is characterized either by in-period or intergenerational discrimination or both. Given the nature of post-constitutional, conflictual politics, each must be (appropriately) constitutionally constrained.

Finally, I emphasize, again, that political, altruistic and moralistic preferences are, on the conservative's account, a legitimate part of the warp and woof of day-to-day conflictual politics. Given that external, like strictly personal, preferences are path-dependent, little can be said *a priori* about which policies and programs may be politically endorsed. If this indeterminancy may be troubling, what is clear is that process matters: Extant and prospective policies and programs must be impartially administered. Given that rent seeking and majoritarian cycling are endemic to representative democracy, it follows that evaluative attention must center on political rather than economic efficiency. While the latter is, in any case, an indeterminate standard (Chapter 4), political efficiency contemplates 'the efficacy of differing institutions in reducing or eliminating the incentive for [conflictual politics'] participants to invest resources in rent seeking aimed to secure discriminatory advantage through majoritarian exploitation' (Buchanan and Congleton 1998, p. 40). It is this understanding - rather than the consequentialist, fundamental theorems of social welfare theory - which animates the work of the constitutional political economist.

Chapter 7, Toward a Conservative Economics, takes as its point of departure the elements of rough correspondence between *homo economicus* and the liberal's conception of the first-person self. Both regard the agent as autonomous and atomistic. Moreover, meddlesome, nosy or external preferences present a particular problem for both construals.

While *homo economicus* is regarded as a narrowly self-interested utility maximizer, it is recognized that, if they are present, interpersonal effects in utility functions are problematic. In particular, if minimal privacy rights are respected, meddlesome or nosy preferences militate against the specification of a social welfare function. This, in turn, calls into question the normative use of the second fundamental welfare theorem. Indeed, the external preferences problem is a metaphor for a larger 'values' problem. *Inter alia*, neither *homo economicus* nor the transcendental, first-person self is informed, animated or constrained by 'ordinary conscience' (Chapter 5).

With this in mind, the balance of Chapter 7 is motivated by three, related ideas: (1) 'No economic theory makes proper sense until conjoined to some adequate political doctrine'. (2) Economic theory must take explicit account of the path-dependency of persons' preference and value structures, and of the endogeneity of formal and informal institutions. (3) Given its Kantian roots, 'conservative' economics must be procedurally-based and consequence-detached. It must, in effect, be the opposite of orthodox, neoclassical economic theory.

The argument suggests, *inter alia,* that the 'theoretical tractability' of the neoclassical paradigm cannot compensate for its inability to account for the endogeneity of preference and value structures, the propensity to cooperate, and the role and importance of formal and informal institutions. Emphasis is placed upon the notion that, if an individual possesses his own strictly personal, external and metapreferences, a 'society with a history' has developed 'historically determined constraints [which] may be descriptively summarized in the laws, institutions, customs and traditions of the community, including the rules or institutions that define the means of making collective "choices"'. Granting this, the focus of interest shifts from choice *within* constraints to the *choice of constraints*. In effect, the problem reduces to this: How might path-dependent, individuated preferences - whether strictly personal, external or meta - be reconciled with the path-dependent formal and informal institutions which characterize 'a society with a history'?

The chapter concludes with an adumbration of the elements of correspondence between the constitutional political economist's research agenda and the conservative's constitutive political position. I conclude that both are informed by the Kantian two-person understanding of the self. It is in this sense that constitutional political economy *is* conservative economics.

Chapter 8 is motivated by the idea, developed in Chapter 7, that the endogeneity of formal institutions, of which law is among the most important, implicates the choice of constraints problem. If this problem - and its solution - finds expression in the conservative's constitutive political position and, *pari passu*, in the work of the constitutional political economist, it animates discussion in the contemporary philosophy of law. At least in one account, 'The issue which stands behind nearly every controversy in contemporary legal theory is the problem of how law is to be understood in relation to moral values'.

Given this predicate, the balance of Chapter 8 concentrates on a critical assessment of three, competing theories of law, and on an adumbration of what may be characterized as a conservative theory of law. A recurring theme, informed by the argument developed in preceding chapters, is that law and morality are inexorably intertwined, and that a proper understanding of that relationship is central to the choice of constraints problem.

The argument suggests that the conceptual part of the 'ruling theory of law' denies objective features of observable reality, while its normative part cannot, logically, generate an obligation to obey the law. For their part, proponents of the Chicago approach take account neither of the irreconcilability of right- and goal-based moral theories, nor of the indeterminancy of the efficiency standard. Finally, the liberal theory deploys a 'rights conception' of the rule of law which asserts that individuals have 'background rights' against external preferences; rights 'which ... hold in an abstract way against decisions taken by the community or the society as a whole'. I argue, *inter alia*, that the rights conception is rooted in a truncated vision of the transcendental, autonomous self. Difficulties arise because neither the justification of, nor respect for, the rights which the theory seeks to protect can be generated by appeal to a self which has no motive to act.

In sharp contrast, the conservative theory of law asserts that the liberal's transcendental autonomous self must be rejected; that 'fundamental liberty interests' are 'rooted in the traditions and conscience of [a] people', and that morality is 'a legitimate state interest'.

NOTES

1. In fact, Rawls' 'difference principle' may be interpreted in this way (1971, pp. 75-83). It should be emphasized, however, that veil of ignorance situated individuals need not choose this principle.
2. This, it seems clear, is precisely what Kant meant in promulgating his 'two points of view' construal:

   > a rational being must regard himself qua intelligence ... as belonging not to the world of sense, but to that of understanding: hence he has two points of view from which he can regard himself, and recognize laws of the exercise of his faculties, and consequently of all his actions: first, so far as he belongs to the world of sense, he finds himself subject to laws of nature (heteronomy); secondly, as belonging to the intelligible world, under laws which being independent on nature have their foundation not in experience but in reason alone. ([1785] 1988, pp. 84-5)

   For more on this, see Rawls ([1989] 1999, pp. 524-25 and 527).
3. This characterization of the Kantian transcendental self is due to Roger Scruton (2002).
4. See also Rawls ([1989] 1999, p. 525).
5. For a similar view of 'perfect freedom', see Mill ([1859] 2000, pp. 75-6).
6. Hans Aarsleff has suggested that 'It is well known that Locke in the *Second Treatise* places the origin of political obligation in the free and contractual passage from the state of nature into civil society' (1994, p. 257). For more on Locke's conception of the social contract, see Ashcraft (1994, pp. 229, 232, 241 and 247).
7. The idea of morality as impartiality can, of course, be expressed through the use of ideal - or impartial - spectators (judges), or veil of ignorance situated impartial contractors (Kymlicka 1993, pp. 193-4).
8. Anthony Quinton has suggested that liberalism has two classic theoretical texts; one is Locke's *Treatise on Government*, the other Mill's *On Liberty* (1995, pp. 247-8).
9. See also Mill ([1859] 2000, pp. 68, 76 and 83-4).
10. See Quinton (1995, p. 250).
11. Jeremy Waldron has suggested that 'Liberals demand that the social order should in principle be capable of explaining itself at the tribunal of each person's understanding' (1987, p. 149). At least in one interpretation, this 'endorsement constraint' gives rise to institutional skepticism. For more on this, see Chapter 5.
12. For a detailed explication of this idea, see Roth (2002, pp. 2-9).
13. In Dworkin's words,'The ultimate justification for these rights is that they are necessary to protect equal concern and respect' (1985, p. 198).
14. See, for example, Dworkin (1978, p. xi).
15. See also Dworkin (1985, p. 198)
16. As we shall see, the same is true of social welfare theory.

2. Derivative Political Positions

2.1 INTRODUCTION

It is clear that liberalism regards utilitarian social welfare theory (SWT) as instrumental to the achievement of its constitutive political position. It follows that SWT plays a central role in liberalism's derivative political positions. This, however, does not exhaust liberalism's utilitarian connection. As we have repeatedly seen, the presence of interpersonal effects in agents' utility functions animates high-minded liberalism's constitutive natural rights construal. Utilitarianism therefore partially defines what liberalism is *and*, at the same time, facilitates the achievement of its 'good ends'. Granting this, 'Liberalism's Utilitarian Connection' merits discrete, extended treatment (Chapter 4).

With this as background, my interest centers on what, at a cross-section of time, may be construed to be uniquely derivative political positions. It should be emphasized, however, that liberalism's derivative political positions are mutable:

> distinct liberal settlements are found when, for one reason or another, those moved by [a] constitutive morality settle on a particular scheme of derivative positions as appropriate to complete a practical liberal political theory. ... Such settlements break up, and liberalism is accordingly fragmented, when these derivative positions are discovered to be ineffective, or when economic or social circumstances change so as to make them ineffective, or when the allies necessary to make an effective political force are no longer drawn to the scheme. (Dworkin 1985, p. 186)[1]

While it is understood that liberalism's 'settlements' or derivative positions are responsive to contingent circumstance, this much can be said *a priori*: Whatever the nature of the extant derivative position(s), it (they) must be regarded as instrumental to the achievement of the good ends defined by the constitutive position. It is clear, then, that from the liberal's perspective, society's formal and informal institutions must promote equality and serve 'as a means to the end of individual freedom' (Scruton 2002, p. 38).[2] The tolerance imperative (S 1.6) is, in an important sense, a metaphor for these good ends. Roughly paraphrased, the autonomous, transcendental, first-person self must be given moral and political space.

As has been emphasized, this conception may be traced to Mill's *On Liberty* (S 1.3) and, more generally, to the Romantic tradition:

> If the authentic self was defined largely through its autonomy from the collective standards of social propriety and aesthetic judgement, then conformity to collective expectation was a measure of the self's distortion and even corruption. In principle, anything that repressed emotion, constricted individual autonomy, or violated the individual's expressive freedom undermined the development of the self's natural endowments and capabilities. (Hunter 2000, pp. 218-19)

While the quotation invokes the past tense it captures the essence of high-minded liberalism's constitutive political position. If the high-minded liberal does not deploy Mill's despotism of custom totem, neither does he embrace Mill's nuanced view of the legitimate intrusion of societal norms (S 1.3). What he does embrace is a rights against external preferences construal which, in turn, reflects the antecedent claim of equality-driven ethical neutrality (S 1.4). It follows that, whatever else is said, the liberal is committed, in his derivative political positions, to the promotion of institutions and policies which, in turn, promote moral (and political) pluralism.

Of particular interest is the symbiosis between liberalism's constitutive moral pluralism and the ethical neutrality of secular psychology. I shall argue that it is this symbiosis which accounts for the liberal's commitment - as a derivative political position - to the educational establishment's 'psychological strategy'. While more will be said of this below (S 2.3), it is sufficient for the moment to emphasize that

> the psychological strategy tends to dismiss (often with ridicule) the idea that there is any content-filled moral agenda we should pass on to succeeding generations. The task, rather, is to give children the wherewithal to sort out the vast number of competing moral claims that confront them. ... the moral individual is one who somehow transcends time, space, relationships, and culture altogether but serves some thin notions of the common good when he or she freely chooses. (Hunter 2000, p. 11)

That this psychological educational strategy 'typically appeals to liberals' (p. 11) should come as no surprise. That I regard it as problematic should also, by now, be apparent.

2.2 SOME THOUGHTS ON MORAL PLURALISM

I do not wish to overstate my case against liberalism's constitutive moral neutrality or pluralism. First, I appreciate that Dworkin acknowledges that rights are not absolute trumps against external preferences:

> Rights may be absolute. ... Rights may also be less than absolute; one principle might have to yield to another, or even to an urgent policy with which it competes on particular facts. We may define the weight of a right, assuming it is not absolute, as its power to withstand such competition. It follows from the definition of a right that it cannot be outweighed by all social goals. We might, for simplicity, stipulate not to call any political aim a right unless it has a certain threshold weight against collective goals in general. (1978, p. 92)

In Dworkin's account, 'the surface antagonism between rights and collective welfare [is] the product of a political theory that is unified at a deeper level' (1978, p. 367):[3]

> I suggest that particular political rights, *and* the idea of the collective welfare, *and* the idea that these function as antagonists at the level of political debate, are all consequences of the fundamental ideal of a political community as a community of equals. (p. 368)

That high-minded liberalism acknowledges that rights are non-absolute trumps against considerations of collective welfare[4] does not, however, alter the fact that 'the right to personal moral decisions' or the 'right to the liberties described in the Constitutional Bill of Rights' are 'derivative, not from a more abstract general right to liberty as such, but from the right to equality itself' (p. xiii).

With this as background, it is precisely the right to equality animated right to personal moral decisions which motivates this chapter.

To frame the discussion, I stipulate first that Dworkin acknowledges that rights are not absolute, and that 'one right is more important than another if some especially dramatic or urgent collection justification ... will defeat the latter but not the former' (p. 366). It follows that, in principle, political, moralistic, or altruistic preferences may prevail against the right to affect personal moral decision making. This requires, however, that a competing social goal outweigh the right to personal moral decisions. Second, I stipulate that, because its constitutive political position is grounded in the 'right to equality itself', the imperative to be tolerant of personal moral decisions is not reflective of a commitment to meta-ethical relativism. This follows from the fact that the latter

> often takes the form of a denial that any single moral code has universal validity, and an assertion that moral truth and justifiability, if there are any such things, are in some way relative to factors that are culturally and historically contingent. (Wong 1993, p. 442)

Yet, if high-minded liberalism cannot embrace meta-ethical moral relativism, it is clear that it must endorse normative relativism. In its most extreme form, normative relativism asserts that 'no one should ever pass judgement on others with substantially different values, or try to make them conform to one's own values' (p. 447). If this were the position adopted by high-minded liberalism, little more would need be said. In this extreme form, normative relativism

> is an indefensible position. It requires self-condemnation by those who act according to it. If I pass judgment on those who pass judgment, I must condemn myself. I am trying to impose a value of tolerance on everyone, when not everyone has that value, but this is not what I am supposed to be doing under the most extreme form of normative relativism. (p. 447)

It follows that, if high-minded liberalism is to avoid self-condemnation, it must endorse a less extreme version of normative relativism. This 'more reasonable' variant 'would have to permit us to pass judgment on others with substantially different values' (p. 448). While he seeks to be non-judgmental, it seems clear that this form of normative relativism gives the liberal what he needs: *Inter alia*, it provides 'a set of reasons for tolerance and non-intervention that must be weighted against other reasons' (p. 449). Among these reasons, it would seem, are 'other values of ours [which] are at stake' (p. 448), and 'dramatic or urgent collective justification[s]'. The latter, in turn, contemplates 'collective welfare' or 'social goals'.[5]

If high-minded liberalism may be characterized as embracing a nuanced form of normative relativism, the same cannot be said of the eduational establishment. I shall argue that, in their rush to disseminate the liberal's tolerance message, some of the proponents of the 'psychological strategy' have adopted meta-ethical moral relativism.

2.3 THE PSYCHOLOGICAL STRATEGY

In his 1998 book, *One Nation, After All*, Alan Wolfe, the Director of Boston College's Center for Religion and American Public Life, concluded that America is a single nation that embraces certain 'transcendental moral principles', but that Americans are reluctant to judge people by applying them. In his 2001 book, *Moral Freedom*, Wolfe seeks, *inter alia*, to understand why this is so: 'I therefore conducted in-depth interviews with people chosen from eight distinct communities, each of which was presumed to present a particular slice of American experience' (p. 4). He concludes, somewhat peculiarly, that 'Like democracy, the arrival of moral freedom is bound to have consequences we will regret. But if we appreciate political and economic freedom, we will have to find a way to appreciate the moral freedom that cannot help but accompany it' (p. 231). Yet, he says of his respondents:

> Listening to the way our respondents talk gives a certain amount of credibility to those who argue that contemporary Americans have too much freedom for their own good ..., our respondents are guided by subjective feelings more than they are by appeals to rational, intellectual, and objective conceptions of right and wrong. It is not standards of excellence to which they turn, but what seems best capable of avoiding hurt to others. They do not think that virtue consists in subsuming their needs and desires to the authority of tradition. Indeed, some of them are not even sure that virtuous is what they want to be. Without firm moral instruction, Americans approach their virtues gingerly .... since they are wary of treating moral principles as absolutes, they reinvent their meaning to make sense of the situations in which they find themselves. (p. 223)

While, admittedly, the quotation is lengthy, it is heuristic. I note, in particular, the allusion to 'subjective feelings', to the avoidance of hurt to others, and to the disinclination to accept the authority of tradition or to treat moral principles as absolutes. Indeed, Wolfe adds that:

> Were Immanuel Kant or Emile Durkheim to appear in America today, he would find little support for the categorical imperative or the collective conscience among our respondents. What so many philosophers and theologians for so long considered an impossible idea [moral freedom] has become the everyday reality in which Americans live. (p. 223)

If Wolfe contends that 'So broad is the current complaint against moral freedom ... that it is no longer the sole property of theological and political conservatives', he is quick to add that 'the underlying message of putting one's needs first has survived' (p. 221). Moreover, he suggests that 'No longer [is] society the conscience ... that [constrains] the individual; now the individual [is] all and society the obstruction' (p. 216). And finally, 'In an age of moral freedom, moral authority has to justify its claims to special insight' (p. 226).

While I am disinclined to engage in hyperbole, it seems clear that moral freedom is, in part, reflective of a disinclination to accept the 'despotism of custom'. Stated differently, it is reflective of what Roger Scruton has called institutional skepticism. In his account, this skepticism is emblematic of 'principles at work in the liberal mind':

> in all questions of law and morality there is room for debate, and ... the onus of proof lies upon the person who would retain some precept rather than upon the one who would have it abolished. The liberal is the one to ask 'why?' of every institution. (2002, p. 71)

Characteristically,

> In all its variants, and at every level, liberalism embodies the question: 'Why should *I* do *that*?' The question is asked of political institutions, of legal codes, of social customs - even morality. And to the extent that no answer is forthcoming which proves satisfactory to the first-person perspective, to that extent we are licensed to initiate change. (p. 186)

At this stage, one might plausibly ask, What has this to do with the educational establishment's psychological strategy? To focus the discussion I return, once again, to Wolfe:

> In the spirit of the 1960s, educational reformers began to advocate radical changes in their institutions, proposing that schools should stop disciplining students, encourage free-form expression and individual creativity, deemphasize honor classes and tracking, and find new ways to teach such subjects as math and history. In extreme versions of educational reform, moral anarchy rather than moral freedom seemed to be the operating principle. (2001, p. 228)

I suggest, first, that the 'educational reforms' to which Wolfe refers are animated by the liberal's constitutive political position. How else might one account for the not-so-subtle embrace of the liberal's 'reforming spirit' (Scruton 2002, p. 174), the invocation of the perfectibility of the autonomous self, and the commitment to moral freedom? I argue, in short, that the educational establishment's psychological strategy is derivative of the liberal's constitutive position. The strategy, in turn, is based on the ethical neutrality of secular psychology:

> Its working assumption is that all of us possess an innate capacity for moral goodness; character resides within each of us, largely independent of the relationships we have or the communities into which we are born. These endowments only need to be coaxed out and developed within the personality. (Hunter 2000, p. 10)

Roughly paraphrased, what is envisioned is nothing less than the nurturing of the liberal's transcendental, autonomous, first-person self. In this account, morality is, quite literally, endogenously determined - freed of intrusion by the despotism of custom, tradition and the 'web of attachments' into which the individual is born.

If Hunter sees the psychological strategy's 'appeal [as] the fantasy of political and religious neutrality', and 'Its conceit ... that it benefits everyone and it offends no one' (p. 10), the liberal view is quite different:

> This vision ... seeks to use education ... to enable each student to resist and overcome social and cultural repression, and hence to authorize his or her own moral voice. (Tappan and Brown 1989, p. 204)

Considered *in vacuo* the passage appears to go beyond Dworkin's nuanced normative relativism. Whereas the latter suggests that the right to personal moral decisions may, in principle, by outweighed by other values or 'dramatic or urgent collective justifications', the Tappan-Brown view comports more closely with meta-ethical moral relativism. It must be said that, if this is representative of secular psychology's ethical neutrality *in practice*, its proponents confront a daunting logical problem: If children are taught that each must be unqualifiedly tolerant of others' 'moral voices' it follows that passing judgment on those who are not tolerant implies that those who affect this judgment must condemn themselves. As we have seen, this is an indefensible position (S 2.2).

If one were asked to distill the psychological strategy - the deployment of the ethical neutrality of secular psychology in the moral education of children - to one word, it seems plausible to suggest that the word would be 'tolerance', 'inclusion' or 'diversity'. Semantics aside, the psychological strategy enterprise is a manifestation of the liberal's tolerance imperative. Whatever else is said, the project is subject to what Hunter has called the 'paradox of inclusion':

we strive to be *inclusive*, taking great pains not to offend anyone by imposing beliefs and commitments. ... This requirement of inclusiveness ... is reinforced by the dominant educational establishment and the state through their policies of nondiscrimination. ... This tension between accommodating diversity in public life and establishing a working agreement in our moral life is a defining feature of our national life. (2000, p. 9)

It is clear that the paradox arises *because* the psychological strategy is derivative of liberalism's constitutive political position: The transcendental first-person self envisioned by the strategy is, indeed, autonomous - 'so much so as to exclude the possibility of commitments that go beyond subjective choices or obligations that are antecedent to personal choice' (Hunter 2000, p. 187).

2.4   THE CONSERVATIVE VIEW

Amitai Etzioni has suggested that roughly two-thirds of all Americans hold that society is in a moral crisis (2001, p. xviii). Relatedly, James Davison Hunter notes that 'Polls show that about 85 percent of all public school parents want moral values taught in school', and, significantly, that 'about 70 percent want education to develop strict standards of "right and wrong"' (2000, pp. 3-4).

Set against this apparently unambiguous call for 'some manner of cohesiveness in the morality we pass on to children' (p. 9) is the liberal's tolerance imperative (S 1.6). The latter is derivative of the liberal's constitutive political position; of the view that the state must be neutral on the question of what constitutes the good life.[6] Whatever else is said, the paradox of inclusion discussed in Section 2.3 is indicative of the tension between the two imperatives.[7]

It is clear that the educational establishment's response has been to ignore the first, and to promote the second imperative. The pedagogy of choice, the ethical neutrality of secular psychology, emphasizes the autonomy of the transcendental, first-person self. The pedagogy does not, however, contemplate a veil of ignorance situated moral agent. The imperative which emerges is not categorical; it is not the Kantian Moral Law: Others are not ends in themselves; instead, the self is an end in itself:

Historically and cross-culturally it is a given that a society's ethical system rested, to one degree or another, upon a code of renunciation. One had to renounce the self and its appetites in order to contribute ... to the common good, to remain faithful to one's spouse, to defend the honor of one's family name, to prepare for battle. In the psychological pedagogies, renunciation is at best an incidental part of the moral imagination. Where it remains possible, it is always provisional, always subject to reevaluation according to the expressive or utilitarian needs of the sovereign self. Its implicit ethic, then, is one of release from the inhibited compulsions or controls within the culture. ... the therapeutic ethos creates a moral logic of fulfillment rooted in the satisfaction of needs and desires. ... In this, the moral imagination is shaped not by communal purpose or collective ideals of transcendent good but by a commitment to personal well-being. (Hunter 2000, p. 192)

Clearly, something has gone wrong. In the conservative view, the problem emerges at two levels. First, the vision of the transcendental, first-person self promulgated by secular psychology's proponents finds no counterpart in the Kantian/Rawlsian construction. Whereas Kant and Rawls imagine a transcendental self ensconced behind a veil of ignorance, the liberal and, *pari passu*, secular psychology imagine a self which is transcendent in the peculiar sense that it is freed of the despotism of custom, tradition and the web of social attachments. And, whereas Kant insists that 'A good will is good not because of what it performs or effects, not by its aptness for the attainment of some proposed end, but simply by virtue of volition' ([1785] 1988, p. 18), secular psychology promotes a commitment to personal well-being.[8] Second, while the morality envisioned both by the liberal and by secular psychology's advocates is self-generating and self-referencing, morality, for the conservative, is informed by ordinary conscience (S 1.5): Whereas there is nothing to which secular psychology's transcendental self has a duty to submit, the conservative imagines that the self, as agent, is both animated and constrained by the Moral Law, by the ethic of virtue, by sympathy, and by piety (Scruton 1996, p. 120). In this account, the perspective of the transcendental first-person self is cultivated by the web of attachments into which a person is born (the third-person perspective) (p. 192).

That the conservative's two-person self comports both with Kant's 'two points of view' ([1785] 1988, pp. 84-5)[9] and with Adam Smith's civilizing project (S 1.3) is both interesting and important (S 3.2). On the one hand, it suggests that the Kantian autonomous self - properly construed - has no analogue, either in the liberal's constitutive political position, or in the secular psychology enterprise. On the other hand, it underscores the role and importance of a 'compelling collective discipline capable of regulating social life' (Hunter 2000, p. 191):

The motive of morality is complex. Were we immortal beings, outside nature and freed from its imperatives, the moral law would be sufficient motive. But we are mortal, passionate creatures, and morality exists for us only because our sympathies endorse it. We are motivated by fellow-feeling, by love of virtue and hatred of vice, by a sense of helplessness and dependence which finds relief in piety, and a host of socially engendered feelings which have no place in the serene dispensations of a 'Holy Will'. (Scruton 1996, pp. 124-5)

The socially engendered feelings to which Scruton refers both cultivate the Moral Law and enable the agent, immersed in contingent circumstance, to answer the questions he must inevitably ask: Why should I do that? Why should I be good? Why should I be impartial? As Hunter suggests, 'moral cultures, in their particularity, provide specific explanations for the "whys" of moral behavior' (2000, p. 22). Granting this, moral education should, to paraphrase Hunter, be more about conformity with social norms than about transformation.[10]

For the conservative, there is no paradox of inclusion. Questions of right, duty and justice as impartiality implicate the Kantian Moral Law. They are the province of the *Kantian* first-person self. But if the Moral Law 'neither forbids nor permits an action, there is still the question whether a virtuous person would permit it' (Scruton 1996, p. 125). The answer to this question implicates the third-person perspective. Informed by the ethic of virtue, sympathy and piety this perspective is itself cultivated by path-dependent social bonds; by the normative order or moral culture into which the moral agent is born. Given the symbiotic relationship between the Kantian first-person perspective and the determinants of the third-person perspective - the latter nurture the first - there is no paradox of inclusion. If, indeed, parents want education to develop strict standards of 'right and wrong' they must recognize the ethical neutrality of secular psychology's pedagogy for what it is: A dangerous and corrosive misinterpretation of the Kantian Moral Law. It is tautological that the *deus ex machina* of 'cohesion in the morality we pass on to children' is not ethical neutrality. It is the cultivation, through society's formal and informal institutions, of the practice of ordinary conscience. Subsuming as it does both the endogenous and the exogenous sources of moral argument and appraisal, ordinary conscience is not 'nonjudgmental'. If, by invoking the Moral Law, the ethic of virtue, sympathy and piety, the practice of ordinary conscience answers the question 'Why should I do [not do] that?', it also develops standards of right and wrong (S 5.4). In the end, ethical neutrality is not an option.

2.5   DIVERSITY

An adumbration of the conservative's critique of the educational establishment's psychological strategy necessarily implicates a variant of liberalism's tolerance imperative:

> The ethic of nonjudgmentalism promoted by *diversity* demands more than just keeping one's invidious judgments to oneself; it is a profound inner commandment that one not make such judgments in the first place. (Wood 2003, p. 150)

Diversity in the sense of multiculturalism evolved from what could be characterized as the affirmative action enterprise. As originally conceived, affirmative action contemplated a college 'admissions program that discriminates in favor of blacks' (Dworkin 1978, p. 239). Following a now familiar line of reasoning, Dworkin suggests that

> The arguments for an admissions program that discriminates against blacks are all utilitarian arguments, and they are all utilitarian arguments that rely upon external preferences in such a way as to offend the constitutional right of blacks to be treated as equals. (p. 239)

In sharp contrast, he suggests, the arguments for an affirmative action program

> are both utilitarian and ideal. Some of the utilitarian arguments do rely, at least indirectly, on external preferences ... but the utilitarian arguments that do not rely on such preferences are strong and may be sufficient. The ideal arguments do not rely upon preferences at all, but on the independent argument that a more equal society is a better society even if its citizens prefer inequality. (p. 239)

If the passages just quoted highlight the role of equality and external preferences in the liberal's constitutive political position, they also underscore the liberal's commitment to good ends or social goals. Here, affirmative action is a derivative political position. It is, in short, instrumentally important to the achievement of a 'more equal society'. In this account, the 'constitutional right of blacks to be treated as equals' trumps the external preferences of citizens who 'prefer inequality'.

As it happens, the passages appeared at roughly the same time as the United States Supreme Court's June 1978 decision in *Regents of the University of California v. Bakke*. Reduced to its essentials, the Supreme Court's decision affirmed the California Supreme Court's order that Allan

Bakke, a white applicant, be admitted to the University's medical school. In affirming the California Court's order, five of the nine Supreme Court Justices held that the University's affirmative action plan was unconstitutional because it denied Bakke the equal protection guaranteed by the Fourteenth Amendment. However, Justice Powell differed from the other four Justices (Brennan, White, Marshall and Blackmun) in holding that 'universities may take race into account explicitly as one among several factors affecting admission decisions in particular cases, in order to achieve racial diversity in classes' (Dworkin 1985, p. 305). In effect, Powell held that the social goal of achieving diversity may trump the right to equal protection under the law.

It should be clear that Justice Powell's construction is consistent with Dworkin's view of rights as non-absolute trumps against social goals (S 2.2). While this is true, in principle, Dworkin finds the 'argumentative base of [Powell's] decision to be weak' (1985, p. 309):

> The constitutionality of an affirmative action plan ... depends, according to Powell, on its purpose as well as its structure. It is not altogether plain how courts are to decide what the purpose of a racially conscious admissions program is. (p. 309)

Granting this, Powell's argument

> does not supply a sound intellectual foundation for the compromise the public found so attractive. The compromise is appealing politically, but it does not follow that it reflects any important difference in principle, which is what a constitutional, as distinct from a political, settlement requires. (p. 309)

Despite his reservations about the 'argumentative base' of Powell's decision, it is clear that Dworkin endorses the idea that the due process right may be trumped by a social goal:

> [Affirmative Action] programs rest on two judgments. The first is a judgment of social theory: that the United States will continue to be pervaded by racial divisions as long as the most lucrative, satisfying, and important careers remain mainly the prerogative of members of the white race. ... The second is a calculation of strategy: that increasing the number of blacks who are at work in the professions will, in the long-run, reduce the sense of frustration and injustice and racial self-consciousness in the black community to the point at which blacks may begin to think of themselves as individuals who can succeed like others through talent and initiative. (p. 294)

Given these two 'judgments', Dworkin concludes that 'It is therefore the worst possible misunderstanding to suppose that affirmative action programs are designed to balkanize America, divided into racial and ethnic subdivisions' (p. 294). Indeed, in his account, 'If we must choose between a society that is in fact liberal and an illiberal society that scrupulously avoids formal racial criteria, we can hardly appeal to the ideals of liberal pluralism to prefer the latter' (p. 295).

Notice, first, how the argument for affirmative action moves *from* the position that the 'constitutional right of blacks to be treated as equals' trumps the external preferences of citizens who 'prefer inequality' *to* the idea that a social goal - a 'more equal society' - can trump the individual right to equal treatment under the law.[11] While it is not clear - at least to me - how this move can be sustained, this much is clear: What Dworkin seeks to do is to appeal to the 'ideals of liberal pluralism' - the notion that government must both treat citizens equally while remaining neutral on questions of the good life and institutionalize a system of non-absolute *individual* rights against external preferences - to rationalize a system of *group* preferences.

The system of group preferences which Dworkin endorses finds contemporary expression in the concept of diversity:

> Diversity ... is above all a political doctrine asserting that *some* social categories deserve compensatory privileges in light of the prejudicial ways in which members of these categories have been treated in the past and the disadvantages they continue to face. (Wood 2003, p. 5)

Equally important, and consistent with Dworkin's view that 'blacks may begin to think of themselves as individuals who can succeed like others through talent and initiative',

> Diversity is not merely a reformulation of the idea of equal access to [Rawlsian] social goods; it is also an attempt to redefine the goods themselves. The idea of diversity is that once individuals of diverse backgrounds are brought together, a transformation will take place in people's attitudes. ... Diversity will breed tolerance and respect, and, because it increases the pool of skills, ... will contribute to economic prosperity. (pp. 5-6)

With the question of the implications of 'group identity' momentarily deferred, my interest centers on the nexus between diversity and the liberal's tolerance imperative. It is clear that the diversity principle calls on us to be nonjudgmental. To accept diversity is, after all, to avoid the work of moral and political judgment: 'Imagining a world in which oppression has been banished is sweet, and to realize that such a world can be brought about by the essentially passive acceptance of quotas and preferences makes it sweeter still' (Wood 2003, p. 304). Indeed, if the educational establishment's moral freedom project focuses on the sovereign individual, it also celebrates group diversity. For a generation, school children have been taught that 'we derive our basic identity from the groups into which we were born'; that we should 'celebrate group differences' and, 'eventually, that American history is a story of dominant whites oppressing other groups' (p. 303).

The juxtaposition of the liberal's autonomous, transcendental first-person self and an imperative to derive one's 'identity' from group attachment is, on the face of it, incongruous. That the two ideas are incommensurable - in the liberal's own terms - should be obvious: Either the individual is transcendental in the liberal's sense - freed that is, from the despotism of custom, tradition and the web of social attachments - or he is immersed in contingent circumstance. It is clear that, if the individual derives his 'identity' from group attachment he is, *pari passu*, subject to the web of attachments into which he has been born. Granting this, the diversity imperative cannot, logically, be derivative of the liberal's constitutive political position. If, to paraphrase Dworkin, diversity is a compromise which the public found attractive, it is most appropriately characterized as an *ad hoc* extension to *groups* of liberalism's *individuated* tolerance imperative.

There is another sense in which the diversity imperative may be irreconcilable with the liberal's constitutive position. It seems clear that the preference for others' group identity is, itself, an external preference. If so, the liberal must face the obvious question: Does the autonomous, transcendental first-person self's right to equal treatment trump others' preference that he find his identity in group attachment? So far as I know, this question has never been addressed.

If the liberal's first-person self cannot, logically, be deployed to derive the diversity imperative, what of the true Kantian perspective? As is well known, Kant insisted that 'Whatever has reference to the general inclinations and wants of mankind has a market value'. In contrast, 'that which constitutes the condition under which alone anything can be an end in itself, this has not merely a relative worth i.e., value, but an intrinsic worth, that is *dignity*' ([1785] 1998, p. 64). It follows that the intrinsic worth or dignity of man finds its basis in 'autonomy' (p. 65). Given his autonomy,

> man and generally any rational being *exists* as an end in himself, *not merely as a means* to be arbitrarily used by this or that will, but in all his actions, whether they concern him or other rational beings, must be always regarded at the same time as an end. All objects of the inclinations have only a conditional worth, for if the inclinations and the wants founded on them did not exist, then their object would be without value. (pp. 56-7)

While it is clear that Kant's ethics are not preference-based (Rawls [1989] 1999, pp. 502, 508 and 527) - a matter taken up in Chapter 4 - the central importance of autonomy is immediately clear. Simply stated, the idea of group identity is alien to Kantian ethics. Indeed, as I have shown, the idea of group identity cannot, logically, be derived from the liberal's individuated constitutive political position. If this is correct, it follows that diversity's group identity project is both irreconcilable with Kantian ethics, and an *ad hoc* imperative unrelated to the liberal's conception of autonomy. Equally important,

> Pursued as a social policy, *diversity* is a form of systematic injustice and it makes us accomplices to injustice. To treat people as objects, as though they are the residuum of their race, class, gender and other such superficialities, and not individuals who define themselves through their ideas and creative acts - that is injustice. (Wood 2003, p. 47)

If diversity is unjust - in the true Kantian sense - it is also self-contradictory:

> [there is a] contradiction between the diversiphiles' insistence that the differences among cultural traditions are vast and irreconcilable, and their simultaneous assertion that diversity is a path to overcoming division and achieving national (or pan-national) unity. (p. 96)[12]

What, then, is the conservative's view of the diversity enterprise? It is apparent, first, that artifically engendered group identity is, in the conservative's account, inimical to social cohesion. As Wood has emphasized,

> The diversiphiles hope to replace America's live-and-let-live pluralism with a respect-my-group-or-else pluralism. And the kind of respect that is demanded is exemplified by the Church of Diversity: I must show that I regard your group as, in every respect, the full moral equivalent of my own. Anything less would imply that

I secretly harbor the judgment that your group is not good enough - and that way, say the diversiphiles, lies oppression. (pp. 168-9)

In effect, '*diversity*-speak provides a cover for a program of radical cultural change in the direction of authorizing a structure of permanent ethnic and victim-group preferences' (p. 221). In this view, the diversity project is a reflection of the liberal's 'reforming spirit', a propensity which 'constitutes a threat, not only to the state, but also to society. The spirit of reform has been too much concerned with private "rights", and not enough concerned with the public order and private duties that make them possible' (Scruton 2002, p. 175). Recall, moreover, that the diversity imperative is animated by the idea that a *social* goal - a more equal society - can trump the *individual* right to equal protection under the law.[13] While the logic of the move from the liberal's constitutive political position (which regards individual rights as trumps against external preferences) to the diversity construal is not clear, this much can be said: The persistent invocation[14] of Justice Powell's stand-alone elevation of diversity to a compelling state interest is an example of liberals' attempts 'to remake the nation through statute, and to substitute statute wherever possible for common law, even in defiance of natural justice' (Scruton 2002, p. 57).

While the tension between natural and social justice is addressed in Section 3.4, it is sufficient for present purposes to note that, whereas liberals regard social justice as a good end, the conservative regards natural justice as a procedural notion. Whereas social justice is the desideratum of the liberal, the conservative insists that natural justice is a 'process of reflection recognized (but not always obeyed) by everyone in their mutual dealings, a process without which no human intercourse would be conceived in the spirit of friendship' (Scruton 2002, p. 78). In this view, natural justice has 'no application to a state of affairs as such, judged independently of the agency which produced it' (pp. 79-80).

The point is precisely that the individuated equal concern and respect which the liberal seeks cannot be achieved through the institutionalization of group rights. Rather, the true, Kantian first-person perspective – the view of individuals as ends in themselves – is cultivated by family, by friendship and by other social bonds. The sense of personal responsibility toward others – of the imperative to treat others with equal concern and respect - is the product of ordinary conscience (S 5.4). Stated differently, natural justice - in the sense of just dealing - is animated by the Moral Law, by the ethic of virtue, by sympathy and by piety (S 1.5). Just dealing, in this account, is not the product of statutory law or a reforming spirit. Rather, the propensity toward natural justice, of personal responsibility toward others, is an inherited, cultivated trait. In contrast, the liberal's diversity project rejects the idea of personal responsibility and substitutes an entitlement. His social justice construal looks 'back at a history of injustices that must be permanently atoned and forward to a future not of racial equality but of "minority majority" dominance' (Wood 2003, p. 278). Social justice, then, contemplates intergenerational discrimination: It seeks, above all, to remediate past injustices by imposing costs on current and future generations. For its part, group identity 'reinforces the dehumanizing habit of judging people by stereotypes' (Wood 2003, p.135) rather than as individuals. This dehumanizing habit is clearly incommensurable with the Moral Law. How, after all, are *individuals* to be treated with equal concern and respect when they derive their identity from the group with which they are associated? From the conservative's perspective, this is decisive. The promotion of group identity and entitlement is corrosive not only of the social bonds which make rights protection and justice possible, but of the individuated equal concern and respect which the liberal so values.

NOTES

1. For a discussion of what Dworkin characterizes as the 'last liberal settlement', see 1985, p. 187.
2. See Chapter 1 for an adumbration of high-minded liberalism's equality and rights construals. Because rights determine the distribution of freedom I employ the term 'freedom' as a proxy for liberalism's rights as trumps against external preferences construction.
3. This suggests, *inter alia*, that my characterization of high-minded liberalism as a hybrid moral theory is correct (S 1.4).
4. See (1978, pp. 232-8) for Dworkin's discussion of 'What is meant by average or collective welfare'.
5. The discussion suggests that high-minded liberalism's tolerance imperative is a form of moral relativism rather than of ethical subjectivism. The latter is a theory that, 'in making moral judgments, people are doing nothing more than expressing their personal desires or feelings. On this view, there are no moral facts' (Rachels 1993, p. 432). I suggest that, because its tolerance imperative is based on a prior ethical commitment to the moral equivalence of persons, liberalism cannot endorse ethical subjectivism. The reason is clear: 'The idea that we ought to be tolerant is itself a [subjective] moral judgment, and subjectivism does not mandate the acceptance of any particular moral judgment, including this one' (p. 443). Variants of ethical subjectivism are equally unavailing. For a discussion of 'simple subjectivism', of 'emotivism', and of the view that 'while moral judgments express feelings, not just any feelings will do', see Rachels (1993, pp. 435-40).
6. Etzioni has suggested that the question of whether it suffices 'to create and maintain a well-formed and nourished civil society to make for a good society, one that we find virtuous' is, for the liberal, the wrong question. For the liberal, 'society ought not to be formulated by a shared understanding of the good' (2001, p. xxi).

7. In Hunter's account, Americans who want education to develop bright line standards of right and wrong are conflicted: 'We say we want a renewal of character ... but we don't really know what we ask for ... We want character but without unyielding conviction ... we want moral community without any limitations to personal freedom' (2000, p. xv).

8. Rawls is clear that the priority of right and the Kantian perspective ensure that 'The parties [in the original position] regard moral personality as the fundamental aspect of the self. They do not know what final aims persons have, and all dominant-end conceptions are rejected' (1971, p. 563).

9. See footnote 2, Chapter 1.

10. For a succinct and powerful discussion of what the ethical neutrality of secular psychology has actually wrought, see Hunter (2000, pp. 146-7).

11. In effect, 'equal protection, as an individual civil right, is imploded when you elevate diversity to a compelling state interest' (Parks 2003, p. B13).

12. Indeed, in *Hopwood v. Texas* (1996), the US Court of Appeals for the Fifth Circuit found that 'Diversity fosters, rather than minimizes, the use of race' (Parks 2003, p. B12). It is difficult to see how the explicit or implicit use of race or any other of an array of social identity desiderata has as its corollary national unity.

13. See, especially, footnote 11.

14. See for example, Higginbotham and Bergin (2003).

3. Equal Treatment, Natural Rights, and Social Justice

3.1 NEUTRALITY AS A THEORY OF THE GOOD

In the concluding section of his essay, 'Liberalism', Ronald Dworkin asks the question, 'What is to be said in favor of liberalism?' While he does not explicitly answer the question, he suggests that 'I do not suppose that I have made liberalism more attractive by arguing that its constitutive morality is a theory of equality that requires official neutrality amongst theories of what is valuable in life' (1985, p. 203). While this may be true, my interest centers on the objections which, as Dworkin acknowledges, his argument will provoke. I am concerned, in particular, with the notion that liberalism 'is self-contradictory because liberalism must itself be a theory of the good'. Dworkin's answer is straightforward: 'Liberalism is not self-contradictory: the liberal conception of equality is a principle of political organization that is required by justice, not a way of life for individuals' (p. 203).

I agree that liberalism's constitutive political position is grounded in a conception of justice as equal treatment. But it is not a Kantian/Rawlsian conception. While the latter is a theory of the right - in the sense that it does not interpret the right as maximizing the good (Rawls 1971, p. 30) - the liberal's equal treatment by government construal incorporates both a theory of the right - of what government ought to do - and a theory of the good.[1]

Consider, first, that the institutional or procedural imperatives to which the Kantian Moral Law give rise are formal rather than substantive. They specify neither which rights (duties) are to be respected, nor what, precisely, equal treatment means (S 1.1). Moreover, the Kantian/Rawlsian equal treatment construal 'does not depend on the realization of the object of the action, but merely on the *principle of volition* ... without regard to any object of desire' ([1785] 1988, pp. 24-5). In this account, 'All theories of individual and social ethics that are focused on the concept of happiness must capitulate before the ideal of absolute obligation and timeless validity in the theory of justification' (Kersting 1992, p. 356).[2]

47

Whatever else is said, the institutional imperatives to which the Kantian Moral Law give rise do not contemplate the promotion of good consequences (Rawls 1971, p. 31). While more will be said of this in Chapter 4, the essential point is that the liberal's equal treatment construal, a concept of the right, implicates the satisfaction of what I shall characterize as 'sanitized' or non-external preferences - a concept of the good.[3] As Dworkin has suggested, liberalism

> is anxious to protect individuals whose needs are special or whose ambitions are eccentric from the fact that more popular preferences are institutionally and socially reinforced, for that is the effect and justification of the liberal's scheme of economic and political rights. (1985, p. 204)

I emphasize, first, that the force of the rights which liberalism seeks to protect 'derives simply from the fact that the first premiss for Dworkin's theory is the right to equality rather than anything else' (Waldron 1995a, p. 17). It is this sense that liberalism's constitutive political position incorporates a theory of the right. But it is also, as the Dworkin quote suggests, consequentialist. It is tautological that the 'special needs' and 'ambitions' which are to be protected against 'more popular preferences' are understood to be arguments of agents' preference or utility functions. While the former are construed to be personal, the latter are, in the liberal's account, interpersonal or 'external':

> On Dworkin's view, rights are taken to be safeguards introduced into legal and political morality to prevent the corruption of the egalitarian character of welfarist calculations by the introduction of what he calls 'external preferences'. (Waldron 1995a, p. 17)[4]

While it is possible to argue that welfarist calculations are not egalitarian,[5] the essential point is that, by invoking what Waldron has called a 'utilitarian framework' (p. 17), liberalism deploys a utilitarian theory of the good.[6] It seems to me indisputable that, for liberals, utilitarianism is appealing because, 'by running everything through people's preferences and interests more generally, it is non-committal as between various more specific theories of the good that people might embrace, and it is equally open to all of them' (Goodin 1993, p. 242). It is precisely because utilitarianism seeks to promote the satisfaction of disparate preferences or interests that it is both a theory of the good and reconcilable with liberalism's tolerance imperative (S 1.6).

Now it must be said that Dworkin denies that liberalism is 'based on some form of preference-utilitarianism' (1985, p. 204). He argues, in particular, that liberalism 'does not make the content of preferences the test of fairness in distribution' (p. 204). But there is an important sense in which this misses the point. It is clear, after all, that his theory of legislative rights is based on a prior ethical commitment to 'the right to equality'; an antecedent right which, he argues, must inform legislative rights, *inter alia*, to affect 'personal moral decisions' (Dworkin 1978, pp. xii-xiii). The rights as non-absolute trumps against external preferences construal is, in this account, not concerned with distributional issues. Rather, its focus is the satisfaction of 'sanitized' or non-external preferences. Granting this, it follows that liberalism's constitutive political position incorporates a theory of the good. It may also be argued that liberalism's constitutive position incorporates a form of rule - rather than preference utilitarianism.[7] While rule-utilitarianism is itself problematic, that discussion is deferred to Chapter 4.

If, as I have suggested, liberalism's constitutive political position does incorporate a theory of the good it *is* self-contradictory. On the one hand, liberalism rejects the conservative view that treating human beings as equals requires a theory 'of what human beings ought to be' (Dworkin 1985, p. 191). On the other hand, it insists that society must promote the satisfaction of sanitized or non-external preferences. This, it seems clear, *is* a view of 'what is valuable in life'. Granting this, liberals cannot reject the conservative view because it deploys a theory of the good life. In fact, liberals reject the conservative view because they have their own theory 'of what human beings ought to be'.

3.2   THE TRANSCENDENTAL SELF MISCONSTRUED

If the liberal's constitutive political position is self-contradictory, it also deploys a truncated vision of the transcendental, autonomous self (S 1.4). Reduced to its essentials, liberals imagine a Kantian-inspired first-person self. In this account, the autonomous self, freed of contingent circumstance, exercises his right to personal moral decisions. While this construal seeks both to explain the value of freedom and to 'define the sphere of privacy within which the individual resides' (Scruton 2002, p. 184), it misconstrues the Kantian image of the transcendental first-person self.

It is true that Kant regards 'a free will and a will subject to moral laws [as] one and the same' ([1785] 1988, p. 78). But it is also true that he acknowledges that

> It must be freely admitted there is a sort of circle here from which it seems impossible to escape. ... we assume ourselves free, in order that in the order of ends we may conceive ourselves as subject to moral laws: and we afterwards conceive ourselves as subject to these laws, because we have attributed to ourselves freedom of will: for freedom and self-legislation of will are both autonomy, and therefore are reciprocal conceptions. (p. 82)

At issue is a simple question: If, on the one hand, the autonomous self is free because it is subject to the Moral Law and, on the other hand, the autonomous self must be under the Moral Law because it is free, how can the moral law be binding? Stated differently,

> Why should I attach such supreme value to moral action and feel in this a personal worth in comparison with which pleasure is to count for nothing? Why should I take an interest in moral excellence for its own sake? (Paton 1964, p. 42)

Kant argues that, in the face of this latent circle, 'what makes categorical imperatives possible' ([1785] 1988, p. 86) is the

> One resource [which] remains to us, namely, to inquire whether we do not occupy different points of view when by means of freedom we think ourselves as causes efficient *a priori*, and when we form our conception of ourselves from our actions as effects, which we see before our eyes. (p. 82)

Kant's 'two points of view' construal is central to his enterprise.[8] In his account, we are subject, as agents, to 'heteronomy' (p. 62) in the sense that any action which springs from desire, emotion or interest is heteronomous (Scruton 1982, p. 65). That said, 'when we conceive ourselves as free we transfer ourselves into the world of understanding as members of it, and recognize the autonomy of the will with its consequence, morality' ([1785] 1988, p. 85). It follows that Kant's conception of an autonomous agent

> is an agent who is able to overcome the promptings of all heteronomous counsels, such as those of self-interest and desire, should they be in conflict with reason. Such a being postulates himself as a 'transcendental being' in that he defies the causality of nature and refers the grounds of his actions always to the 'causality of freedom'. (Scruton 1982, p. 65)

Significantly, while Kant acknowledges that the latent circle ([1785] 1988, p. 85) is unavoidable, so that while we 'could never solve it through theoretical reason, ... practical reason assured us only that it *has* a solution' (Scruton 1982, p. 66):

The practical use of common human reason confirms this [two points of view] reasoning. There is no one, not even the most consummate villain ... who, when we set before him examples of honesty of purpose, of steadfastness in following good maxims, of sympathy and general benevolence (even combined with great sacrifices of advantage and comfort), does not wish that he might also possess these qualities. ... He proves by this that he transfers himself in thought with a will from the impulses of the sensibility ... since he cannot expect to obtain by that wish any gratification of his desires ... he can only expect a greater intrinsic worth of his own person. This better person, however, he imagines himself to be when he transfers himself to the point of view of a member of the world of the understanding, to which he is involuntarily forced by the idea of freedom ... from this point of view he is conscious of a good will ... a law whose authority he recognizes while transgressing it. (Kant [1785] 1988, p. 87)

Kant insists, then, that the transcendental first-person self cannot, by itself, provide a motive to respect the Moral Law. Agency and, *pari passu*, subjection to the strictures of the categorical imperative require immersion in contingent circumstance. While this means that the self cannot *be* transcendental, it also means that examples of honesty, steadfastness, sympathy and benevolence can cultivate the transcendental perspective. In Kant's words, 'What he morally "ought" is then what he necessarily "would" as a member of the world of understanding, and is conceived by him as an "ought" only inasmuch as he likewise considers himself as a member of the world of sense' ([1785] 1988, pp. 87-8). In more contemporary language, Kant's two person point of view 'is able to give us some purchase' on the latent circularity which Kant recognized:

It is impossible that I should *be* a transcendental self; but it is necessary that I should suffer the illusion that I am. If I am to be fulfilled at all, I must belong to a world in which this illusion can be sustained, so that my projects are also values for me, and my desires are integrated into a vision of the good. There is, therefore, a third-person justification for the first-person perspective. (Scruton 2002, p. 192)

In this true Kantian account, immersion in contingent circumstance both provides a motive to act and, given examples of honesty, steadfastness, sympathy and benevolence, develops the transcendental, first-person perspective. Importantly, the 'ought' which emerges from this perspective is not the 'abstract, universal "ought" of liberal theory - or, at least, not yet - but the concrete immediate "ought" of family attachments. It is the "ought" of piety, which recognizes the unquestionable rightness of local, transitory and historically conditioned social bonds' (p. 192).

This, it seems to me, captures the essence of Kant's two points of view construal. Adoption of the first- *and* third-person perspectives results in the emergence of 'an entire system of common-sense morality [predicated] on the premise of transcendental freedom' (Scruton 1982, p. 67). It must be said, however, that this common-sense morality is not congruent with the abstract, universal 'ought' of liberal theory (Scruton 2002, p. 192). Indeed, whereas Kant and conservatives regard the third-person perspective as necessary both to animate action and to *develop* the Kantian first-person perspective, the liberal seeks to immunize the transcendental first-person self from the intervention of others' external - or moralistic, altruistic or political - preferences (Dworkin 1978, p. 235). It follows that, in his single-minded commitment to an abstract, universal 'ought' - the moral sovereignty of the transcendental first-person self - the liberal either misconstrues or ignores the Kantian two-person point of view. Equally important, by denying (or ignoring) the force and effect of Kant's 'latent circle' the liberal does not address the question of agency. The resulting paradox of liberalism is itself debilitating (S 1.5). And, finally, his rights as non-absolute trumps against external preferences construal is corrosive of the conditions which nurture the true, Kantian first-person perspective.

In short, the liberal's transcendental self construal is neither Kantian nor internally consistent.[9] In sharp contrast, the conservative's two-person perspective is both Kantian and congenial to the development of the true, Kantian first-person perspective (Chapter 5).

3.3 THE LIBERAL'S NATURAL RIGHTS PROJECT

As we have seen, Ronald Dworkin's explanation of the values which underlie liberalism's natural rights construal relies upon persons' fundamental right to equal treatment. Given this Kantian antecedent, rights are regarded as non-absolute trumps against welfarist calculations which are informed by external preferences (Waldron 1995b, p. 582). While, as Waldron has suggested, this does not explain the trumping force of rights against non-welfarist social goals, it is nevertheless true that liberalism's natural rights construal unfolds 'within a utilitarian framework' (1995a, p. 17). As we shall see (Chapter 4), this 'utilitarian connection' is itself problematic. Reduced to its essentials, the problem arises because 'we have no reason to believe that a utilitarian would be obliged to respect the moral force of justified *legal* rights and obligations' (Lyons [1982] 1995, p. 136).[10]

If the inability of utilitarianism to accommodate the moral force of rights suggests that liberalism's natural rights construal is internally inconsistent, account should also be taken of Jeremy Bentham's ontological objection to the concept of natural rights. In his *utilitarian* account, 'the language of natural rights ... "is from beginning to end so much flat assertion: it lays down as a fundamental and inviolable principle whatever is in dispute"' (Waldron 1995b, p. 581).[11]

Whatever else is said, it is clear that liberalism's attempt to reconcile its theory of the right with a utilitarian theory of the good (S 3.1) is open to question. That said, my interest centers on the question of natural rights considered *in vacuo*.

As Margaret MacDonald has suggested, 'the claim to "natural rights" has never been quite defeated' ([1947-1948] 1995, p. 21). The notion that rights may be antecedent to civil society may be traced to John Locke and, more broadly, to the contract theory of the state (S 1.3). In this account, '"natural" rights attach, by virtue of his reason, to every man much as do his arms and legs. He carries them about with him from one society to another' (p. 27).[12]

What are we to make of this claim? First, while I associate myself with the Kantian idea of the moral equivalence of persons - an ethical commitment which can properly be regarded as antecedent to civil society - I acknowledge that

> It is the emphasis on the individual sufferer from bad social conditions which constitutes the appeal of the social contract theory and the 'natural' origin of human rights. But it does not follow that the theory is true as a statement of verifiable fact about the actual constitution of the world. The statements of the Law of Nature are not statements of the laws of nature, not even of the laws of an 'ideal' nature. For nature provides no standards or ideals. All that exists, exists at the same level, or is of the same logical type. There are not, by nature, prize roses, works of art, oppressed or unoppressed persons. Standards are determined by human choice, not set by nature independently of men. (pp. 30-31)

Granting this, 'Assertions about natural rights ... are assertions of what ought to be as the result of human choice' (p. 34). In this account, 'natural rights' cannot be antecedent to civil society. Rather, they are *political* claims asserting that

> In any society and under every form of government men ought to be able to think and express their thoughts freely; to live their lives without arbitrary molestation with their persons and goods. They ought to be treated as equal in value, though not necessarily of equal capacity or merit. (p. 33)

It should be emphasized that the *political* character of 'natural' rights means, on the one hand, that the character and content of rights - and, it should be said, of rights restrictions - reflect the 'fundamental values of a society' (p. 35). On the other hand, the promulgation of legal rights may also be *informed* by the Kantian Moral Law.

In the first instance, the fundamental values of society will, themselves, reflect the 'legacy of custom and prejudice, and ... contingent circumstance of [localized] human history' (Scruton 2002, p. 187). Granting this, the body of law and, *pari passu*, institutionalized rights, are not - indeed, cannot be - the exclusive province of transcendental, first-person selves.[13] Rather, legal rights reflect the *agency* of third-person selves immersed in contingent circumstance. Insofar as the web of social attachments 'leads people to see the world in terms of value, and so to develop the [true Kantian] first-person perspective' (Scruton 2002, p. 192), legal rights will come, also, to reflect the Moral Law. It is in this sense that an emergent rights structure is not congruent with Lockean 'natural' rights. Instead, legal rights may be construed to reflect both heteronomy *and* 'the autonomy of the will with its consequence, morality'. In short, both the rights structure and, importantly, the rights restrictions embraced by civil society reflect Kant's 'two points of view' (S 3.2).

A number of conclusions emerge from this analysis. First, rights cannot properly be construed to be 'possessed antecedently to all specific claims within an organized society' (MacDonald [1947-1948] 1995, p. 21). It follows that rights which are construed to be non-absolute trumps against external preferences are not natural rights. Rather, the construal reflects a claim - whose legitimacy may be questioned - which is animated by a misunderstanding of the true, Kantian first-person self (S 3.2). Second, it is clear that the rights structure extant at any cross-section of time cannot be determined *a priori*. This is true, both because the structure is path-dependent, and because 'the list of natural rights varies with each exponent' (p. 31).[14] If path-dependency is a corollary of the influence of changing contingent circumstance, rights proliferation reflects the fact that the liberal vision of freedom 'seems a permanent feature of the American political and constitutional tradition' (Sandel 1996, p. 5):

> The version of liberalism that puts the right before the good finds its clearest expression in constitutional law. More explicitly than any other institution, the Supreme Court presides over the priority of right, in both senses of that priority. First, it defines the rights that constrain majority rule. Second, it tries to identify these rights in a way that does not presuppose any particular conception of the good. (p. 28)

While these ideas are more fully developed in Chapters 5 and 8, the essential point is that, in America, the liberal imperative to give moral and political space to the transcendental, autonomous self has largely displaced the long dominant view that 'liberty depends on sharing in self-government'. In the latter account, a view which comports with the conservative tradition,

> self-rule ... requires that citizens possess, or come to acquire, certain qualities of character, or civic virtues. But this means that [conservative] politics cannot be neutral toward the values and ends its citizens espouse. The [conservative] conception of freedom, unlike the liberal conception, requires a formative politics, a politics that cultivates in citizens the qualities of character self-government requires. (pp. 5-6)

For the moment, the point is not that the liberal's natural rights construal dominates American jurisprudence. Neither is it the point that, as Scruton has suggested, liberalism it the 'official ideology of the Western world' (2002, p. 182). Rather, it is that, in contrast to the conservative view, the liberal's constitutive political position defines liberty 'in opposition to democracy, as a constraint on self-government' (Sandel 1996, p. 25). A defining characteristic of the project is that, in denying a role for external preferences, it contributes to a metastasization of rights *against* majority rule. Given that the imperative to protect the natural 'freedom' of the sovereign individual is formal rather than substantive, this should come as no surprise.

Consider, first, H.L.A. Hart's thesis that 'if there are any moral rights at all, it follows that there is at least one natural right, the equal right of all men to be free' ([1955] 1995, p. 77). Even if one were to grant that this right *can* be antecedent to civil society - and so to deny the Kantian two-person point of view - it is not clear what, precisely, it entails. Given the inherent fungibility of the natural rights idea, it is apparent that all manner of 'rights' may be rationalized.[15] If the liberal's constitutive rights as non-absolute trumps against external preferences construal comes to mind, so, too, does the generalized 'right of privacy that protects from governmental interference such personal activities as marriage, procreation, contraception, and abortion' (Sandel 1996, p. 91).

If rights proliferation is a problematic corollary of the natural rights idea, that is not the fundamental problem. Rather, the key objection to its natural rights construal attaches to liberalism's attempt to justify rights from a truncated Kantian first-person perspective. In this account the transcendental 'first-person viewpoint constrains the agent to recognize objective rights, and to recognize also the equal entitlement of all agents who are, like himself, blessed with a first-person perspective' (Scruton 2002, p. 188). The problem is that, as Kant acknowledged, what makes the categorical imperative possible is a two-person perspective (S 3.2). Roughly paraphrased, veil of ignorance-generated principles of justice do not bind the agent once the veil is removed. Stated differently, *respect* for the equal treatment imperative, and for the 'objective rights' which liberalism so reveres requires immersion in contingent circumstance.[16] If, in short, the true Kantian first-person perspective is to be respected, it must be cultivated: 'we must conserve the institutions, customs, and local attachments through which the first-person perspective of the liberal is nurtured ... the attachments, being founded not in abstract justice, but in ... "natural piety", are corroded by the very liberal conscience which they generate' (p. 193):

> The predicament of liberal democracy in contemporary America recapitulates the tensions that inhabit its ideals. Far from proving the autonomy of liberal politics, its practice confirms what its philosophy foretells: The procedural [liberal] republic cannot secure the liberty it promises, because it cannot sustain the kind of political community and civic engagement that liberty requires. (Sandel 1996, p. 24)[17]

The contradiction reduces to this: Whether the rights which it seeks to protect are characterized as natural or political, nothing in liberalism's constitutive political position generates an imperative to respect them.[18] In denying or ignoring the role and importance of Kant's two-person point of view, liberalism 'is doomed to corrode the conditions which nurture it' (Scruton 2002, p. 193).[19] Respect for rights - however construed - requires appeal to a first- and third-person perspective. But this, as we shall see (Chapter 5), is a conservative perspective.

3.4 NATURAL AND SOCIAL JUSTICE

If respect for rights requires a two-person point of view, the same is true of natural justice. Natural justice is, above all, a procedural concept:

> The principal application of 'natural justice' is to human actions, and, by extension, to the character from which those actions spring. It has no application to a state of affairs as such, judged independently of the agency which produced it. The sense of justice, ... arises only because we can see the justice of individual actions, and feel drawn towards the will from which they spring. If, at some later stage, we come to extend the idea, and

speak of the justice or injustice of social and political relations we mean to refer, not to their nature, but to their cause. (Scruton 2002, pp. 79-80)

In this account, an 'instinctive conception of what is just' (p. 79) is reflective of the workings of ordinary conscience (SS 1.5 and 5.4). Insofar as reciprocal dealings are informed by the four sources of moral argument and appraisal '"just dealing" arises naturally between people' (p. 78). Stated differently, the propensity to treat others as ends rather than as means - the Kantian first-person perspective - is both animated and cultivated by the third-person perspective; by the web of social attachments into which the individual is born. Natural justice, then, is not the 'mere creation of a sovereign power'. It is cultivated, in the manner of ordinary conscience, by 'friendship, benevolence and love' (p. 79).

In sharp contrast, the concept of 'social justice' finds its genesis in the institutional skepticism and reforming spirit of the high-minded liberal (S 1.4). While he is committed both to the economic market and to representative democracy (Dworkin 1985, pp. 193-4), the liberal insists that 'resources and opportunities should be distributed, so far as possible, equally' (p. 192). Granting this, and given 'the anti-egalitarian consequences of free enterprise in practice' (p. 194), the liberal 'lawgiver' seeks to reform the market 'through a scheme of redistribution that leaves the pricing system relatively intact, but sharply limits ... the inequalities in welfare that his initial principle prohibits' (p. 196). Social justice, then, is not a procedural notion. Rather, it is the desideratum of the liberal, egalitarian reformer (Scruton 2002, p. 79).

It is significant that, in his egalitarian enterprise, the liberal regards the state as instrumental to the perfectibility of the market system. Equally important, he imagines that social justice can be achieved by the 'liberal lawgiver's' appeal to the second fundamental welfare theorem or, more broadly, to the economist's theory of the state. While this is the subject matter of Chapter 4, it is sufficient for the moment to note that the theory's fundamental constructs are indeterminate. Granting this, social justice-animated redistribution schemes must be regarded as *ad hoc*.

Considered *in vacuo*, this should be sufficient to give the liberal lawgiver pause. So, too, should his propensity to regard differences in ability and inheritance as producing 'forbidden inequalities' (Dworkin 1985, pp. 195-6). It is, after all, well known that 'The natural distribution [of talents] is neither just nor unjust; nor is it unjust that persons are born into society at some particular position. These are simply natural facts' (Rawls 1971, p. 102). It follows that

> In order to employ this concept of 'justice' in political debate, ... the advocate of 'social justice' creates a peculiar unconscious fiction: the fiction that really all wealth, and perhaps all advantage, belongs to a single owner (society), which (in some inexplicable way) has the duty to ensure its 'distribution'. (Scruton 2002, p. 80)

For the conservative, the imperative is not, and cannot be, the pursuit of social justice or other 'good ends'.[20] In the conservative's account, 'some ends - perhaps the most important ends - remain to be discovered rather than imposed. And in the life of society they are discovered not by the perusal of utopian treatises, but, primarily through participation' (p. 13). The imperative, in short, is not to remake or 'perfect' the state by statute. Rather, it is to ensure that the ethic of natural justice informs constitutional, statutory and common law. This, to be sure, is just another way of saying that the Moral Law, the ethic of virtue, sympathy and piety must be embodied in the law. Thus, if the liberal sees the law - from his transcendental first-person perspective - as a distributor of constitutional rights *against* the state, the conservative - from his Kantian two-person point of view - sees 'constraints on freedom [arising] through the law's attempt to embody (as for a conservative it must embody) the fundamental values of the society over which it rules' (pp. 6-7). Respect for prevailing social values is both a *sine qua non* for the authority of the law, and justificatory of law's intrusion into 'any area of social life which is vital either to the strength of the social bond, or to the social image of its participants' (p. 73). These and related matters are taken up in Chapter 8.

NOTES

1. For more on theories of the right and of the good, see Goodin (1993) and Pettit (1993). See also Rawls (1971, p. 24). It should be noted that Rawls characterizes his Kantian theory of justice as fairness as deontological; as a theory that does not interpret the right as maximizing the good. That said, he insists that 'All ethical doctrines worth our attention take consequences into account in judging rightness. One which did not would simply be crazy' (1971, p. 30). I suggest that this is true of liberalism's constitutive political morality. Interestingly, if Dworkin seems implicitly to deny this, conservatives do not. *Inter alia*, the conservative's ordinary conscience construal (S 5.4) insists that, when the Moral Law speaks, it takes precedence. But, when rights and duties conflict, 'a kind of utilitarian thinking comes into play, as the means to extend our sympathies to all whose interests are affected by our acts' (Scruton 1996, pp. 125-6).
2. See also Rawls (1971, p. 31) and Scruton (1982, p. 73).
3. Recognizing that it is questionable that 'racist, sadistic and other such antisocial preferences should count as contributing to individual well-being', Hausman and McPherson have suggested

that one response is to 'launder' preferences (1993, pp. 690-91). This, it is clear, is Dworkin's approach.

4. See also Dworkin (1978, pp. 234-5).
5. As Rawls has suggested, utilitarianism mistakes impersonality for impartiality (1971, p. 190). I shall have more to say about this in Chapter 4.
6. As Goodin has emphasized, utilitarianism is 'the theory of the good most standardly used to fill out the larger consequentialist framework' (1993, p. 242).
7. For a discussion of rule-utilitarianism, see Lyons (1982, pp. 128-32).
8. For more on Kant's two points of view and the 'vicious circle', on how the categorical imperative is possible, and on the questions of freedom and moral interest, see Paton (1964, pp. 41-52).
9. It has been suggested that Rawls' 'Kantian conception of justice as fairness' does not incorporate Kant's two points of view. See, for example Scruton (2002, p. 191). This may, however, be incorrect. See footnote 18.
10. See also Waldron (1995a, pp. 18-9) and Chapter 4.
11. As is well known, Bentham 'dismissed absolute natural rights as "nonsense upon stilts"' (Almond 1993, p. 266).
12. It should be noted that the natural rights doctrine 'has seemed particularly vulnerable to ethical skepticism'. In this account, 'The idea of *natural* rights is seen as a particularly glaring example of the "Naturalistic Fallacy", purporting to derive certain norms or evaluations from descriptive premises about human nature'. In the face of these epistemological difficulties 'it becomes important, in the area of rights as elsewhere, for philosophers to identify clearly the deep assumptions on which their theories depend' (Waldron 1995a, p. 3). In liberalism's case, natural rights are justified by appeal to a particular - and inappropriate - understanding of Kantian autonomy.
13. As we have seen, agency requires a motive to act. But a motive to act is unavailable to the transcendental, first-person self.
14. More generally, some have suggested that 'the widespread appeal of rights [is] an unwelcome proliferation of a notion which is either suspect or redundant' (Almond 1993, pp. 260-61).
15. Jeremy Waldron (1995b) notes that 'In international human rights circles, diplomats talk about "first-", "second-" and "third- generation" rights'. In this account, first-generation rights are 'the traditional liberties and privileges of citizenship'; second-generation rights are 'socio-economic claims', and third-generation rights 'have to do with communities or whole peoples' (p. 578). Presumably, the group rights contemplated by the 'diversity' imperative fall under the rubric of third-generation rights (S 2.5).
16. As Brenda Almond (1993) has suggested, this is the heart of the conservative objection to the natural rights enterprise (p. 267):

> writers in the conservative tradition object to the individualism implicit in the assertion of rights. They see the individual of Western liberalism as rootless and want to replace the idea of the individual as a social atom with the idea of individuals in their social roles within an organic community.

17. For a similar critique of contemporary (or high-minded) liberalism, see Skinner (1991).
18. Roger Scruton suggests that the contradiction 'may equally be discerned in the "Kantian constructivism" of Rawls. In Rawls' case it takes the following form: granted that, when choosing from behind the veil of ignorance, I choose the abstract principles of justice, what then binds me to that choice once the veil is removed?' (2002, p. 190). While this may be true, it must be said that Rawls' argument does appear to implicate Kant's two-person point of view:

> many applications of the principles of justice are restricted by the veil of ignorance, whereas evaluation of a person's good may rely upon a full knowledge of the facts. ... in judgments of justice, it is only at the judicial and administrative stage that all restrictions on information

are dropped, and particular cases are to be decided in view of all the relevant facts. (Rawls 1971, pp. 448-9)

19. It is clear, moreover, that the idea of rights is inexorably bound up with agency. Indeed Gewirth has argued that agency is the key to rights (1978; 1982, pp. 41-178). Yet the transcendental, first-person self has no motive to act. This is the essence of the liberal paradox (S 1.5).
20. The same might be said of Kant. As Wolfgang Kersting has suggested, 'The principle of equality is indifferent to the economic structure of society; it does not make the advancement of social equality and economic justice a political goal' (1992, p. 356).

4. Liberalism's Utilitarian Connection

4.1   A REPRISE

As has been emphasized, Ronald Dworkin insists that utilitarianism is not constitutive of liberalism (1985, pp. 201-2). In fact, it *is* characteristic of liberalism's constitutive and derivative political positions. On the one hand, the rights as non-absolute trumps against external preferences construal is an attempt to perfect both majoritarian democracy and utilitarianism (Dworkin 1978, p. 277).[1] On the other hand, the liberal's impulse to reform the market system to correct 'forbidden inequalities' (Dworkin 1985, p. 196) implicates the economist's utilitarian theory of the state (SS 1.4 and 3.4). Utilitarianism is, therefore, both an integral part of the liberal's constitutive political position, and instrumental to the achievement of the good ends defined by the constitutive position.

Finally, whatever else is said, it is clear that, because it incorporates elements of right- and consequentialist or goal-based moral theories, liberalism is a hybrid moral theory. While the fundamental irreconcilability of these theories and, *pari passu*, of the logical opposition between liberalism and utilitarianism is the focus of section 4.3,[2] immediate interest centers on an equally fundamental problem. Reduced to its essentials, liberalism's utilitarian enterprise cannot be reconciled with Kantian ethics.

4.2   AT ODDS WITH KANTIAN ETHICS

The Kantian idea of a transcendental first-person self is, as we have seen, the foundation upon which high-minded liberalism is built (SS 1.2 and 1.4). Importantly, in emphasizing the moral and political autonomy of the sovereign first-person self, the liberal enterprise ignores Kant's 'two points of view' ([1785] 1988, p. 82). If this lacuna gives rise to the Paradox of Liberalism (S 1.5), it also misconstrues the Kantian transcendental self (S 3.2).

That said, liberalism's truncated autonomy construal takes no account of the fact that Kant derives his first and second propositions of duty from the transcendental first-person perspective. While Kant acknowledges that agency and the *possibility* of the categorical imperative requires a third-person perspective (S 3.2), he insists that an action done from duty derives its moral worth, *not from the purpose* which is to be attained by it, but from the maxim by which it is determined, and therefore does not depend on the realization of the object of the action ... without regard to any object of desire. ([1785] 1988, pp. 24-5)[3]

It follows that insistence upon a transcendental, first-person perspective - an idea which has been characterized as 'the theoretical cornerstone of liberalism' (Scruton 2002, p. 188) - has a logical corollary: 'All theories of individual and social ethics that are focused on the concept of happiness must capitulate before the idea of absolute obligation and timeless validity in the [Kantian] theory of justification' (Kersting 1992, p. 356). In effect, the veil-of-ignorance - or original position - situated, transcendental first-person self cannot be subject to heteronomy. He cannot, in other words, be subject to such 'external causes' as 'interests, desires and ambitions, and all the "empirical conditions" which circumscribe [his] actions' (Scruton 1982, pp. 65 and 69).[4]

It is clear, then, that liberalism cannot be grounded in the transcendental first-person self and, at the same time, embrace utilitarianism in its constitutive and derivative political positions.   To do so is to be internally inconsistent.[5] Equally important, liberalism's invocation of the economist's theory of the state (S 3.4) is incompatible with Kantian political philosophy.   This is true for the obvious reason that the economist's theory is utilitarian (S 4.4).   But it is also true because 'Kant's political philosophy is decidedly antipaternalistic, rejecting every form of the politics of care for happiness and moral education' (Kersting 1992, p. 356).[6] Thus, while he 'develops an argument against state paternalism' (G. Dworkin 1995, p. 363) which manifests itself in the claim that 'no event or achievement can make a person's life better against his opinion that it does not', Ronald Dworkin nevertheless endorses the idea of the perfectibility of the market system.   In his account, appeal to the economist's utilitarian second fundamental welfare theorem can, in principle, correct 'the antiegalitarian consequences of free enterprise in practice' (Dworkin 1985, p. 194).   What seems not to be appreciated - or, at least, acknowledged - is that this idea and, more generally, the social justice imperative (S 3.4), cannot be reconciled with Kant's antipaternalistic political philosophy.

4.3   THE MORAL FORCE OF RIGHTS

If liberalism's embrace of utilitarianism is logically inconsistent with Kantian ethics and political philosophy, it is also incompatible with the moral force of the legal rights which liberals seek both to justify and to protect. The core problem is that right- and goal-based moral theories are not reconcilable:

> utilitarian arguments for institutional design (the arguments that utilitarians might use in favor of establishing or maintaining certain legal rights) do not logically or morally exclude direct utilitarian arguments concerning the exercise of, or interference with such rights. As a consequence, evaluation of conduct from a utilitarian standpoint is dominated by direct utilitarian arguments and therefore ignores the moral force of justified legal rights. (Lyons 1982, p. 113)[7]

Aware of what he characterizes as the 'surface antagonism between rights and collective welfare', Dworkin suggests that the conflict is the 'product of a political theory that is unified at a deeper level'. In his account, it is the 'fundamental ideal of a political community as a community of equals' (1978, p. 367) which mitigates - but cannot eliminate - the antagonism. It must be said, however, that the proffered 'unification' is unavailing.[8] The liberal view of rights as non-absolute trumps against external preferences does, after all, contemplate the possibility that welfare considerations may outweigh the trumping force of rights (S 2.2). Moreover, as we have seen, respect for rights - however construed - requires appeal to a first - *and* third-person perspective. Yet nothing in liberalism's constitutive position allows for this Kantian insight (S 3.3). That said, it is clear that Dworkin's view that 'moral-legal principles [may be weighed] against considerations of good social policy' (Tebbit 2000, p. 109) cannot be sustained. Insofar as 'good social policy' is animated by utilitarian considerations, 'The problem of establishing the threshold at which pre-existing rights can be outweighed by arguments from social policy is a much larger one than that faced by Dworkin' (pp. 110-11). In effect, utilitarian arguments can always trump the rights which Dworkin seeks both to justify and to protect.[9]

If, as I suggest, the fundamental incommensurability of rights and utilitarianism suggests that liberalism's constitutive political position is logically inconsistent, the same is true of its derivative political position. This is true because, as we have seen, the latter regards the economist's utilitarian theory of the state as instrumental to the achievement of such equality-motivated desiderata as social justice (SS 1.4 and 3.4).

4.4   THE LINK TO THE ECONOMIST'S THEORY OF THE STATE

The economist's theory of the state is effectively summarized by the two fundamental theorems of utilitarian social welfare theory.[10] The first theorem asserts that, *under certain simplifying assumptions*, a perfectly competitive market system will automatically move to a first-best, Pareto-optimal or 'competitive' equilibrium (Novshek and Sonnenschein 1987; Duffie and Sonnenschein 1989). The competitive equilibrium is understood to be a point on the efficiency or welfare frontier. A defining characteristic of the frontier is that, as movement along it proceeds, one agent gains - in a utility sense - at the other's expense. It is in this sense that competitive equilibria are Pareto-optimal or efficient. For its part, the second fundamental theorem indicates that, no matter to which point on the efficiency frontier a perfectly competitive system is automatically impelled, a different, 'socially desired', Pareto-efficient allocation can be realized by appeal to lump-sum taxes and bounties (Graaff 1957, pp. 75-83). Granting this logic, the efficacy of a perfectly competitive market mechanism is preserved:

> The [second fundamental] theorem is widely interpreted as meaning that we can divorce the issue of efficiency from distribution. It is not an argument against markets that the resulting distribution of income is undesirable. If society does not like the distribution of income, the government's distribution branch ... just alters the initial distribution of resources, through lump-sum redistributions. (Stiglitz 1994, p. 45)

Given this characterization of the 'perfectibility' of the market system it is not surprising that the market system and the second fundamental theorem find expression in liberalism's derivative political position (SS 1.4 and 3.4).

4.5   SOCIAL WELFARE THEORY: AN OVERVIEW

I begin by stipulating that utilitarianism is 'first and foremost, a standard for judging public action'. In this account, 'the right action is that which maximizes utility (however construed) summed impersonally across all those affected by that action. ... That is ... the standard that public policy-makers are to use when making collective choices impinging on the community as a whole' (Goodin 1993, p. 245). Because it is outcomes-based and procedurally-detached, utilitarianism is ill-adapted to address questions of institutional design. While, in principle, rule-utilitarianism endorses rules which are justified on utilitarian grounds, utilitarian arguments can always be deployed to deviate from the rules (Roth 1999, p. 39). This, as we have seen, undermines the logic of the liberal's rights as trumps against external preferences construal (S 3.3). Moreover, as we have seen, utilitarian theory cannot accommodate the moral force of rights (S 4.3).[11] Finally, it should be emphasized that the utilitarian justification of democratic institutions is, at best, tentative (Brennan and Buchanan 1985, p. 49). In effect, the only dimension of moral appraisal of political acts is a comparative assessment of their consequences (Davis 1993, p. 205). It follows, *pari passu*, that, rather than seeking to 'get the institutions right', the utilitarian imperative is to promote the public good. The public good, in turn, is understood to exist independently of the expression of individual values. This idea, it should be emphasized, finds expression in the notion of a social preference or welfare function; an idea which is central to utilitarian social welfare theory (SWT).

These ideas inform the economist's normative application of SWT. This, in turn, is a reflection of what Hahn has called the 'relentlessly utilitarian' nature of economic theory's core ontology (1982, p. 187).

Central to the social welfare theoretic enterprise is the distinction between 'efficiency' in the sense of Pareto optimality, and 'equity'. While the former contemplates the efficiency or welfare frontier, the latter implicates the social welfare function. For the moment, our interest centers on the former.

The instantaneously prevailing efficiency frontier is determinate, given the behavioral and technological postulates which characterize the frictionless, neoclassical decision environment:

- Individual consumers are autonomous, atomistic, narrowly self-interested and classically rational utility maximizers. Moreover, preferences are exogenously determined, intertemporally stable, and defined on objects of choice whose technical, qualitative and property rights characteristics are known with certainty.
- Individual producers employ single-equation, flow-flow production functions which, *inter alia*, are assumed to be the only efficient or output-maximizing technical alternatives available.
- Property and exchange rights - which are instrumentally important to the achievement of first-best Paretian optima - are assumed to be

unattenuated. The duties correlative to these rights are, therefore, implicitly assumed to be respected.

• Given these assumptions, and given that all transactions are instantaneous, transaction costs are zero.

• Finally, the theory is both institutionless and intendedly value-free.[12]

Achievement of points on the efficiency frontier - or, what is the same thing, of first-best Paretian optima - is predicated upon satisfaction of three 'welfare conditions'. As is well known, the three conditions are satisfied at long-run perfectly competitive equilibrium. In effect, the fixity of product and input prices ensures satisfaction of the three marginal equivalences and, *pari passu*, the attainment of a Pareto-optimal or efficient outcome. It is on this logic that, given unattenuated property and exchange rights, the first fundamental welfare theorem asserts that a perfectly competitive system will automatically move to a point on the efficiency or welfare frontier. Granting the logic of the approach, 'efficiency' and, *mutatis mutandis*, the first fundamental welfare theorem, become instruments of public policy appraisal. *Ceteris paribus,* violations of one or more of the three welfare conditions constitute 'market failure' and may, therefore, justify government market intervention. In effect, imperfect product and input markets are 'perfectible'.

The competitive equilibrium to which a perfectly competitive system is impelled may or may not be an 'ethical' or 'socially desired' equilibrium (Furubotn 1971). Determination of the latter is, in turn, predicated on the existence of a single-valued, consistently ordered social welfare function.[13] While it must be said that it is by no means clear that the empirical, ontological and other problems attaching to the notional social welfare function can be overcome (S 4.9), I assume for the moment that the function has an empirical counterpart. Granting this - and setting aside the theoretical and empirical difficulties associated with lump-sum taxes and bounties (Graaff 1957, p. 78) - the second fundamental theorem has normative implications: Insofar as the competitive equilibrium differs from the ethical equilibrium, government 'ought' to institutionalize an appropriate redistribution scheme. As in the case of the first fundamental theorem, the second theorem may, therefore, be deployed to 'perfect' the market system. Given liberalism's intellectual commitment to the perfectibility of the market system (S 3.4), SWT's appeal is immediately apparent.

4.6 THE NEOCLASSICAL DECISION ENVIRONMENT

The logic of the efficiency frontier requires that the underlying utility and production functions embody orthodox, neoclassical properties, and that the decision environment be frictionless (S 4.5).[14]

I stipulate, again, that the received, neoclassical theory is both institutionless and intendedly value free. This accounts, in part, for the theory's positivist or instrumentalist methodological orientation. From this perspective, the distinction between generative and auxiliary assumptions is crucial. Whereas the latter specify the parameters of a model, the former impute properties to functional relationships and serve, given the auxiliary assumptions, to generate hypotheses. In the positivist account, whereas generative assumptions need not be realistic, the empirical confirmability (disconfirmability) of an hypothesis depends upon the realism of the auxiliary assumptions. Given realistic auxiliary assumptions, empirical confirmation of a model depends upon the correspondence of predictions with observable reality (Roth 1998, Chapter 1).

Homo economicus is central to the neoclassical paradigm.[15] He is taken to be an autonomous, atomistic agent who seeks to maximize utility subject to exogenously determined constraints. With the intertemporal stability of preferences understood to be an auxiliary assumption, the key generative assumption is classical rationality. In this account, the agent's strictly personal preference structure is consistently ordered and exogenously determined. The objects of choice of the narrowly self-interested agent are taken to be purchasable economic goods whose properties are known with certainty, and whose associated property rights are both well-defined and unattenuated. Finally, it is characteristic of this frictionless decision environment that information asymmetries and opportunistic behavior are absent.

The presumption is, in short, that there is a one-to-one correspondence between the agent's objective and subjectively perceived decision environments. Importantly, because fully informed agents engage in instantaneous, classical contracting, transaction costs and, *pari passu*, the *ex ante* and *ex post* costs of contract enforcement are zero (Furubotn and Richter 1997, p. 142).

While much can be said about this, immediate interest centers on the notion that preference structures are exogenously determined and intertemporally stable.

It is now generally recognized that the classical rationality postulate cannot be tested independently of stability of preferences (Robinson 1962).[16]

While the literature characterizes the associated inability to confirm (disconfirm) model predictions as reflecting the presence of an unidentified exogenous variable, more is ultimately at issue. Reduced to its essentials, the problem is that preference structures are endogenously determined (Buchanan 1994b, pp. 76-7). It is recognized, for example, that evolutionary[17] and other path - dependent phenomena[18] influence preference and value structures.[19] These path dependencies may, in fact, account for the anomalous behavior which is judged to be inconsistent with classical rationality (Tversky and Thaler 1990). Anomalous behavior may, in short, reflect the intervention of learning, of social norms, and of higher-order preferences, or preferences-for-preferences (North 1994).[20] Equally important, decision processes may be complicated by internal conflict; by such interpersonal (and other) effects as altruism, sympathy, piety, and the desire for self-approbation.[21]

If it is possible to question the presumed exogeneity and stability of preferences, it is also possible to question the empirical content of the classical rationality postulate (Simon 1992, p. 3).[22] The essential idea is that, whereas for *homo economicus* there is no gap between his competence and the difficulty of the decision problem to be solved, cognitive limitations characterize the boundedly rational decision maker (Conlisk 1996).[23] If there is no generally accepted definition of bounded rationality, there is agreement that it implies what Heiner (1983) has called a competence-difficulty (C-D) gap. Given this understanding, constrained optimization of any sort is 'a special case occurring when uncertainty (the C-D gap) approaches zero' (Wilde, LeBaron and Israelsen 1985, p. 403).

Among the defining characteristics of boundedly rational agents' decision environments are information asymmetries. Broadly speaking, individuals differ with respect to their stocks of knowledge, their ability to process extant and incremental knowledge, and their ability to disentangle the effects of environmentally generated random events, and those effects which are the result of opportunistic behavior (Williamson 1985, p. 47). If the interaction of bounded rationality, random events and opportunistic behavior implies that property and other rights may not be respected (Furubotn 1994, p. 25), it also underscores the role and importance of ethical norms.

While these considerations are incommensurable with the *homo economicus* construal, they have a long history in economics. It is clear, for example, that Adam Smith recognized the reciprocal nature of preference and value structures, and the setting within which such structures are shaped (S 1.3).[24] Smith recognized both 'The influence of Custom and Fashion upon Moral Sentiments' ([1759] 1976, pp. 200-211) and, through his concept of self-approbation (p. 114), the existence of multiple preference and value domains.

If the 'positivist revolution' - and, *pari passu*, SWT - are incompatible with Smith's view, empirical findings in evolutionary psychology comport with his thinking.   Roughly paraphrased, utility derives from the consumption of comestibles. But it also derives from self-reference, from helping and hurting others, from caring about others as 'ends', from interpersonal relationships, and from setting goals and achieving them (Aaron 1994, p. 15).

Whatever else is said, it is clear that the path-dependent, multiple preference domains just adumbrated cannot be represented by an intertemporally stable, exogenously determined, single-equation utility function.   Simply stated, economic man's motivation is too narrowly construed (Klamer 1989, p. 147).[25]

The single-equation utility function has an analog in neoclassical production theory (S 4.5). The theory deploys a single-equation, flow-flow production function which is assumed, *inter alia*, to be the only 'efficient' or output maximizing technical alternative available to the firm. This assumption, in turn, requires that, as movement along the short-run expansion path proceeds, the capital stock which generates the fixed service flow adapts itself perfectly and instantaneously to changing rates of use of the variable service flow(s).[26] A patently unrealistic generative assumption, perfect adaptability is justified on the logic that the purpose of the model is prediction rather than explanation.

While, in principle, this methodological posture is unassailable (Roth 1998, Chapter 1), the perfect adaptability assumption leads to a logical conundrum: As perfect adaption proceeds, the physical form of the capital input changes. It follows, *pari passu*, that each point on the short-run expansion path is associated with a differentiated form of the capital input type employed. Yet, as the physical form of the capital input type changes, the technical properties of the associated 'fixed' service flow must change. The corollary is that perfect adaptation of the capital input type implies that the production function must change. Granting this, movement along the neoclassical short-run expansion path is a logical impossibility (Roth 1974).

If the logic of the neoclassical short-run expansion path is internally inconsistent, the same is true of the long-run expansion path. While the latter contemplates a decision environment in which capital stocks and, therefore, production functions change, the long-run expansion path is defined for an *unchanging* production function.

These considerations suggest that, for logical and empirical reasons, the firm's 'technology' cannot be represented by a single-equation, efficient, flow-flow production function. In most cases of practical importance, the output of any product may be secured via the employment of differentiated forms of human and nonhuman capital input types. It follows that, within and across industries, production functions may properly be characterized as multi-equation constructs (Roth 1979). In the situation envisioned, each production subfunction or production technique has as its parameters particular differentiates of the capital input types employed.

Assume, for example, that the production of product '*A*' contemplates the employment of capital input types K_1 and K_2. On the presumption that the capital stocks appear, respectively, in $j = 1, 2, ..., m$ and $k = 1, 2, ..., n$ differentiated forms we understand that each of the K_{1j} and the K_{2k} generates a unique, technologically distinct service flow denoted, respectively, x_{1j} and x_{2k}. It follows that the multi-equation, stock-flow production function for product '*A*' may be written

$$A_t = g_i (x_{1jt}, x_{2kt} \mid K_{1j}, K_{2k}) \tag{3.1}$$

where $i = 1, 2, ..., s$
and $s = m \bullet n$

The logic of system (3.1) suggests that each of the s production subfunctions has as its parameters differentiates of the capital stocks, K_1 and K_2. Thus production subfunction g_1 has as its parameters K_{11} and K_{21}. The physical and technical properties of K_{11} and K_{21}, in turn, determine the technical properties of the associated service flows, x_{11}, and x_{21}, employed per unit time, t.

While system (3.1) is, at best, heuristic, it nevertheless captures the essence of the 'choice of technique' problem: Given its desideratum, which of these production functions or 'techniques' should A's producer employ?[27] On the plausible assumption that producers, like consumers, are boundedly rational, and that transaction and decision costs are positive, two conclusions emerge.[28] First, the boundedly rational producer cannot, at a cross-section of time, be presumed to have exhaustive knowledge of the technical array which confronts him (Furubotn 1999, p. 183). The plausibility of this conclusion is underscored once account is taken of extant and potential technical interactions among production complexes, and of the number of capital input types typically employed.[29] Second, it is tautological that the producer must decide *how to choose* among his *subjectively perceived* technical options. Yet, this lower-order problem contemplates both positive decision costs *and* an infinite regress problem. In effect, one must decide upon the decision process by which a decision rule is to be selected. But this begs the question, How was the prior decision process selected? The problem has a logical corollary:

> decision costs act to limit the extent to which rationality can be displaced to higher levels. There must come a point where, as Knight says, the 'rational thing to do is to be irrational' and simply choose a choice method without reason. Otherwise, all resources would be used in decision-making. (Pingle 1992, p. 11)

It seems clear, then, that the decision environment contemplated by neoclassical production theory is irreconcilable with objective features of observable reality. Contrary to the received theory, there is no one-to-one correspondence between the objective, but unknowable, decision environment, and its subjectively perceived counterpart.[30] This is, of course, analytically equivalent to saying that the logic of the firm-subjective production function is not reconcilable with the production-theoretic foundations of SWT. The essential difficulty is that, given bounded rationality and positive decision costs, there can be no presumption that firms within and, *mutatis mutandis*, across industries will employ the same production function - let alone the same service flows. Once this has been said, it is evident that the space in which the production theoretic contract curve might be defined is indeterminate. It follows that the production possibility frontier - a *sine qua non* for the derivation of the efficiency frontier - cannot be derived.

4.7 THE INDETERMINANCY OF THE EFFICIENCY FRONTIER

The argument developed above suggests that fundamental features of observable reality militate against the specification of the efficiency frontier. At issue here is not the oft-cited nirvana fallacy. Whereas the fallacy obtains when the efficiency frontier is employed as a normative benchmark without taking account of real and unavoidable constraints (Roth 2002, pp. 43-52), the problem adumbrated here is more fundamental.

Simply stated, the juxtaposition of bounded rationality and positive decision costs on the one hand, and the complexity of observable reality on the other hand, calls into question the ontological existence of the efficiency frontier.[31]

Whether interest centers on preference and value structures, or on the technological link between outputs and inputs, the familiar logic of contract curve derivation is disturbed. In the case of the former, the interaction of bounded rationality, information asymmetries, path dependencies and the complex nature of individuals' desiderata ensure that individuals will be characterized by disparate preference and value domains.[32] It follows that the arguments of individuals' multi-equation utility functions will differ, and the contract curves which are a *sine qua non* for the derivation of the efficiency frontier are indeterminate.

The argument is symmetrical with respect to the production theoretic foundations of the efficiency frontier. Generation of the frontier is predicated, in part, upon the existence of the production possibility frontier (PPF). Yet the logic of the contract curve from which the PPF is derived requires, *inter alia*, that producers within and across industries employ homogenous productive services. While this is an analytically convenient assumption, it is irreconcilable with a technical environment characterized by bounded rationality, information asymmetries and positive decision costs. In reality, the employment of subjectively determined production functions and, *pari passu*, of heterogeneous service flows, is inconsistent with the derivation of the PPF. It follows that it is not possible to effect a mapping of utility possibility frontiers and, *mutatis mutandis*, of the efficiency frontier.

The implications of the indeterminacy of the efficiency frontier are immediately clear: Appeals to the first fundamental welfare theorem or, what is the same thing, to the so-called 'efficiency standard' are unavailing. Efficiency-animated attempts to 'perfect' the market system contemplate appeal to a normative standard for which no operational counterpart exists. Moreover, even if one were to reject the logic of my ontological objection, account must be taken of Lipsey and Lancaster's 'The General Theory of Second Best' (1956). The 'negative corollary' of the theorem for the second best optimum is that 'it is *not* true that a situation in which more, but not all, of the optimum conditions are fulfilled is necessarily, or even likely to be, superior, to a situation in which fewer are fulfilled' (ibid., p. 12). On this logic, Lipsey and Lancaster suggest that the principles of the general theory of second best show the futility of 'piecemeal welfare economics'. To apply to only a small part of the economy welfare rules which would lead to a Paretian optimum if they were applied everywhere, may move the economy away from, rather than toward, a second best optimum position. (1956, p. 17)

The irremediable fact is, of course, that invocations of the first fundamental welfare theorem are, inevitably, 'piecemeal'. While policy initiatives may, in principle, be informed by general equilibrium theory, explicit account cannot be taken of all of the interrelationships which define an economy (Salanié 2000, p. 18).[33] It follows that there can be no presumption that 'if the market fails, the government is sure to do better' (Sandmo 1990, p. 58).

While more will be said about this in S 4.11, the upshot is that liberals cannot plausibly regard the first fundamental welfare theorem as instrumental to the perfectibility of the market system.

4.8   THE PATH TO THE FRONTIER

The indeterminacy or, more properly, the nonexistence of the efficiency frontier suggests that government policies informed by the first and second fundamental welfare theorems cannot be regarded as 'scientific'. In fact, they may best be characterized as *ad hoc*.

That said, let us suppose for the moment that the frontier *is* determinate. Unfortunately - for those liberals and others who would deploy the theory - fundamental logical problems remain. Contrary to the received view, the path to the frontier, or to first-best Paretian optima, is not assured.

Recall, first, that SWT assigns an instrumental role to unattenuated property and exchange rights (S 4.5). While the theory is outcomes-based and procedurally-detached, the path to the frontier is reliant upon respect for these rights. Yet, as we have seen, the theory is formulated in utilitarian terms. The problem is that utility considerations trump rights (SS 3.3 and 4.3). As Lyons has emphasized, 'evaluation of conduct from a utilitarian standpoint is dominated by direct utilitarian arguments and therefore ignores the moral force of justified legal rights' (1982, p. 113). The corollary is that utilitarian SWT cannot accommodate the moral force of instrumentally important rights. Granting this, it is clear that even if one were to grant its existence, the path to the frontier is compromised.

If the irreconcilability of right- and goal-based theories jeopardizes the path to the frontier - and, therefore, to 'competitive equilibria' - the same is true of neoclassical theory's zero transaction cost assumption (S 4.5). The difficulty is that the assumption leads to a logical conundrum. As

Furubotn (1991) has suggested, a decision environment characterized by costless transactions is congenial to the formation of coalitions which, effectively, rule out the satisfaction of the three conditions for a first-best Paretian optimum.

The upshot is that, even if one grants it existence, logical inconsistencies inherent in SWT compromise the path to the efficiency frontier.

4.9   THE INDETERMINACY OF THE SOCIAL WELFARE FUNCTION

As is well known, the utilitarian social welfare function is understood to be an interest-aggregation decision mechanism which defines the optimal social outcome as the maximization of the sum of individual utilities. It is intended, in short, to be a mechanism for deciding among states of affairs. Familiarly, because it is utilitarian, it presupposes the normative judgment that the standard of outcome evaluation is that the social optimum is that which maximizes aggregate utility or 'welfare' (Roth 2002, pp. 17-19).

Attachment to this understanding of the public or social good has persisted in the face of well established empirical and logical problems. In the first instance, Arrow's Possibility Result (1951) established that, if interpersonal utility comparisons (IUCs) are ruled out, there is no method of aggregating individual rankings of social alternatives which meets five patently innocuous criteria. Yet it is clear that IUCs must be ruled out. As has been emphasized, individuals' preference and value structures are both path-dependent and defined on complex utility domains (S 4.6). It follows that IUCs are possible neither at a cross-section of time, nor intertemporally for the same individual. Moreover, once account is taken of the fact that boundedly rational agents' objectively defined and subjectively perceived decision environments are not congruent, it is clear that IUCs are a *practical* impossibility.[34]

If empirical problems militate against the specification of a social welfare function, so too does a fundamental logical problem. The problem finds expression in Amartya Sen's Paretian liberal construal. In broad outline, the juxtaposition of meddlesome or nosy preferences and *respect* for minimal privacy rights militates against the emergence of any social choice (Roth 1999, pp. 40-41). If, as James Buchanan suggests (1994b, p. 75), such preferences are a palpable reality, the efficacy of the social welfare function as an interest aggregation decision mechanism is called into question. It seems clear that, Professor Sen's efforts to expand the informational base of SWT notwithstanding (Roth 2002, pp. 21-3), the practical impossibility of effecting IUCs and the impossibility of the Paretian liberal are to the social welfare function what bounded rationality, information asymmetries, and positive decision costs are to the efficiency frontier. An explicit accounting of objective features of observable reality renders both constructs indeterminate.

Finally, while empirical and logical questions attend the specification of a social welfare function, a fundamental, ontological question remains unanswered. As James Buchanan has suggested, the idea of 'social preference' imputes 'rationality or irrationality as an attribute of the social group'. In effect, this construal 'implies the imputation to that group of an organic existence apart from that of its individual components' (Buchanan 1954, p. 116). Interestingly, Amartya Sen, who himself suggests that 'the "informational base" of welfarism is too thin to support an acceptable - and perhaps even a coherent - account of the social good' (Sugden 1993, p. 1947), finds this objection 'quite persuasive' when 'social preference' connotes the operation of social decision mechanisms such as voting procedures (Sen 1995, p. 5).

Whatever else is said, it is clear that, in light of its logical, empirical and ontological problems, efforts to deploy the second fundamental welfare theorem both to rationalize and to animate redistribution policies must be regarded as *ad hoc*.

4.10 SOCIAL WELFARE THEORY AND THE DIMENSIONS OF MORAL APPRAISAL

While the implications for liberalism of the indeterminacy of SWT's fundamental theoretical constructs are adumbrated in S 4.11, it is important to recall that liberals regard the second fundamental welfare theorem as instrumental to the achievement of 'social justice'. Motivated by his concern that 'resources and opportunities should be distributed, so far as possible, equally', the liberal seeks to perfect the market system. In particular, he seeks by means of lump-sum taxes and bounties to limit 'the anti-egalitarian consequences of free enterprise' (S 3.4).

It is appropriate, first, to note that social justice is not a procedural notion. Second, even if one were to grant the existence both of the efficiency frontier and the social welfare function, 'To be truly lump-sum a tax must bear no relation whatsoever to a man's effort or earnings'. Given this understanding, 'It is clear that truly lump-sum taxes are extraordinarily hard to devise' (Graaff 1957, p. 78).[35] That said, if I am right that neither the efficiency frontier nor the social welfare function has an operational counterpart, determination of lump-sum taxes and bounties is a moot question. In either event, liberalism's social justice enterprise is complicated by the fact that lump-sum taxes and bounties are either 'extraordinarily hard to devise' or theoretically indeterminate.

With this as background, liberalism's propensity to regard SWT as instrumental to the achievement of *social* justice raises a broader, philosophical question: Can SWT accommodate *any* understanding of justice?

It is, of course, immediately clear that social welfare theorists - and those who deploy the theory - cannot, in the manner of libertarians, regard justice as respect for rights (Nozick 1974, pp. 150-53). The core problem is the inability of utilitarian SWT to accommodate the moral force of rights. As the Nobel laureate social welfare theorist Amartya Sen has emphasized, 'no direct and basic importance is attached in the utilitarian framework to rights and liberties in the evaluation of states of affairs' (1995, p. 13).[36]

If the accommodation of rights, and of justice as respect for rights poses an intractable problem for SWT, so too do other justice construals.

To see this, consider first that SWT does not deploy an explicit definition of justice. The theory is silent about the justice - however defined - both of the 'competitive equilibrium' to which a perfectly competitive system gravitates, and of the initial endowments which, along with relative prices, determine the unique, first-best Paretian allocation.

What, then, of the ethical equilibrium contemplated by the theory? Does it contemplate any plausible understanding of justice? To answer this question I set aside the question of the indeterminacy of the social welfare function (S 4.9), itself a *sine qua non* for the determination of ethical, as opposed to competitive, equilibria. In effect, I assume the existence of a single-valued, consistently-ordered utilitarian social welfare function.

I begin with some preliminary observations. First, it is clear that preference satisfaction may not be an adequate conception of individual and, *mutatis mutandis*, 'social' well being. Preferences may, after all, be based upon false, idiosyncratic, highly contestable or malign beliefs. Moreover, there may be circumstances in which preferences have to be 'laundered' before becoming suitable to be accorded moral weight (Hausman and McPherson 1993, p. 714). This, it is clear, is the essence of the liberal's rights as trumps against external preferences construal. It follows, in any case, that even if the existence of the notional social welfare function is granted, the 'moral weight' of the ethical equilibrium may be called into question. Second, justice - whether of the distributive or the commutative type - is a procedural notion (Scruton 1994, p. 425). It is a concept which, on this understanding, 'makes sense only when applied to the dealings between people' (pp. 424-5). Whatever else is said, it is clear that consequence-based, procedurally-detached social welfare theory is ill-adapted to the accommodation of such a concept.

With all of this as background, two theories of procedural justice have been characterized as the 'leading contenders' (Barry 1989, p. xiii). The first regards justice as mutual advantage, while the second characterizes justice as impartiality. As one of two contemporary contractarian or social contract theories, the former accepts the view that persons are, by nature, equals. However, whereas justice as mutual advantage stresses a 'natural equality of physical power, which makes it mutually advantageous for people to accept conventions that recognize and protect each other's interests and possessions' (Kymlicka 1993, p. 188), Kantian justice as impartiality stresses the moral equivalence of persons.

Whatever else is said, it is clear that justice as impartiality is grounded in Kant's categorical imperative. In this account, the imperative to promote just institutions is respected by veil of ignorance-situated individuals who take no account of contingent circumstance (Rawls 1971, p. 563). It follows that 'good outcomes' are neither defined nor promoted and, in contrast to utilitarian social welfare theory, justice as impartiality starts with a theory of the right, the moral law. It is clear, therefore, that justice as impartiality cannot be accommodated by social welfare theory.

Central to the justice as mutual advantage project is the notion that it is mutually advantageous for persons to adopt conventions against harming each other (Kymlicka 1993, p. 189). The adopted conventions, in turn, constitute the 'social contract' or moral code; a code which is 'generated as a rational constraint from the non-moral premises of rational choice' (Gauthier 1986, p. 4). For its part, the obligation to respect the adopted conventions is grounded in the idea that bargaining proceeds 'among expected utility maximizers with common knowledge of everyone's capabilities, endowments, and preferences' (Hausman and McPherson 1996, p. 158). While this understanding of agents' decision environments is congruent with the neoclassical paradigm (S 4.5), the essential point is that this rich informational base is presumed to be a bargaining constraint: The rational agent is presumed never to agree to accept less than he could obtain in the absence of agreement.

The bargaining constraint is, of course, reminiscent of the logic employed in the derivation of social welfare theoretic contract curves and, therefore, of the efficiency frontier. The notions are not, however, congruent. Because there is no presumption that particular outcomes ought to be promoted, the theory of justice as mutual advantage is not utilitarian or, more generally, consequentialist. It is clear, therefore, that social welfare theory cannot accommodate this understanding of justice.

Granting the logic of what has been said, utilitarian SWT cannot accommodate the libertarian theory of justice as respect for rights. Moreover, neither contractarian understanding of justice is reconcilable with the theory. A corollary of this is that SWT can deploy only one dimension of moral appraisal, Pareto optimality or efficiency. That said, it is important that account be taken of Amartya Sen's attempt to enrich SWT's 'informational base'.

While much can be said about his motivation and approach (Roth 1999, pp. 59-63), immediate interest centers upon Sen's conception of justice. In his view, the agent's capability set, the constraint which determines his opportunity to achieve well-being, provides the most appropriate informational base for a theory of justice. In effect, Sen's theory demands equality of capabilities.

Given the logic of his approach, equal command over 'resources' - in the sense of income and wealth - does not imply equal opportunities in the sense of such 'functionings' as 'being adequately nourished' and 'being happy' (Sen 1992, p. 38). Understood in this way, functionings are an aspect of living, with comestibles merely instrumental to their achievement. A state of being, then, consists in a vector of functionings, and an agent's choice among the set of vectors determines the kind of life he lives. Granting all of this, the set of feasible functioning vectors is the agent's capability set. It is in this sense that the capability set is the constraint which determines the agent's opportunity to achieve well-being.

While Sen's approach has intuitive appeal, it is clear that, if it is to be operational, a metric must exist by which to measure the intrinsic value of functionings and capabilities. The problem is complex. On the one hand, if functionings have intrinsic value, information about agent's contingent preferences and choices is unavailing. On the other hand, if well-being is a 'broad and partly opaque concept' which is intrinsically ambiguous (Sen 1992, pp. 46-9 and 134), it is not clear how such values are to be determined. In view of these difficulties, it is 'natural to ask how far Sen's framework is operational' (Sugden 1993, p. 1953).

It is not clear, then, that Sen has succeeded in expanding the 'moral reach' of utilitarian SWT. While he seeks to 'integrate procedural considerations in consequential analysis' (Sen 1995, p. 13), efficiency remains the only dimension of moral appraisal to which SWT gives rise.

If right-based, contractarian and consequentialist-procedural understandings of justice cannot be accommodated by SWT, the question becomes: Can *any* principle of justice be accommodated? In Robert Nozick's account, the answer is 'Yes':

> Welfare economics is the theory of current time-slice principles of justice. The subject is conceived as operating on matrices representing only current information about distribution. This, as well as some of the usual conditions (for example, the choice of distribution is invariant under a relabeling of columns), guarantees that welfare economics will be a current time-slice theory, with all of its inadequacies. (1974, p. 154)

The essence of Nozick's argument may be expressed in the language of SWT. First, nothing in the theory appraises the morality of the initial endowment or of the property and exchange right structure which, along with relative prices, determines the unique, Pareto-optimal or efficient outcome. Second, the notion that structurally identical distributions are equally just is a corollary of the theory's utilitarian ontology: 'Two distributions are structurally identical if they present the same profile, but perhaps have different persons occupying the particular slots. My having ten and you having five, and my having five and your having ten are structurally identical distributions' (p. 154). While Rawls has suggested that this problem reflects utilitarians' propensity to mistake impersonality for impartiality (1971, p. 190), the essential difficulty is that nothing in the theory justifies this view. The core problem, in short, is that end-state or time-slice principles of justice are unhistoric. The forward and backward myopia inherent in utilitarian SWT implies a principle of justice for which no justification is offered and which, in any case, does not tell the whole story about distributive shares (Nozick 1974, p. 154).

By way of summary, utilitarian SWT cannot accommodate the moral force of rights. It follows, therefore, that it cannot accommodate the libertarian view of justice as respect for rights. Moreover, it cannot accommodate contractarian theories of justice. Finally, the end-state or time-slice principle of justice to which SWT implicitly gives rise is incomplete. It follows, then, that the only standard of moral appraisal to which the theory gives rise is Pareto-optimality or efficiency. Yet, as we have seen, the efficiency standard is itself indeterminate.

4.11 THE IMPLICATIONS FOR LIBERALISM

This chapter took as its point of departure that utilitarianism is characteristic of liberalism's constitutive and derivative political positions. Of particular interest is social welfare theory's instrumental role in the achievement of the 'good ends' defined by the constitutive position. The resulting discussion has demonstrated that

- Its 'utilitarian connection' is not reconcilable with liberalism's Kantian roots.
- Liberalism's rights as trumps construal takes no account of utilitarianism's inability to accommodate the moral force of rights.
- Liberalism's appeal to the first fundamental welfare theorem takes no account of the indeterminacy of the efficiency frontier and, therefore, of the efficiency standard.
- Liberalism's appeal to the second fundamental welfare theorem takes no account of the indeterminacy of the social welfare function.
- Liberalism's social justice imperative takes no account of social welfare theory's inability to accommodate any plausible understanding of justice.

Whatever else is said, it is clear that liberals must either embrace their notion of the Kantian first-person self and reject utilitarianism, or embrace utilitarian impersonality and reject their rights as trumps against external preferences and equal treatment construals. Moreover, the empirical, logical and ontological difficulties outlined above suggest that social welfare theory can serve neither as a 'positive' theory of the state nor as an instrument of normative policy appraisal.[37] It follows that invocations of the first and second fundamental welfare theorems serve neither to 'perfect the market system' nor to promote 'social justice'. Granting this, the *deus ex machina* by which these liberal imperatives might be achieved cannot be the economist's theory of the state.

Finally, there is this. If social welfare theory assumes that 'government' may be modeled as a single, 'benevolent despot' (Buchanan [1959] 1999, p. 203) advised by an omniscient observing economist (Graaff 1957, p. 13), it also ignores the intervention of political institutions (Salanié 2000, pp. 8-9). Setting aside the patent implausibility of the benevolent despot-omniscient observing economist formulation, the essential point is that the model ignores the intervention of political processes which, presumptively, affect and are affected by the self-interest of politicians, bureaucrats, and voter-principals. Once this has been said,

> There is no necessary presumption that simply because markets are imperfect, political processes will work better. On the contrary, as public-choice theory reminds us, there are very good reasons for doubting the capacity of political processes to achieve Pareto optimality. The normatively relevant comparison is between two imperfect institutions. The mere observation that one institution or the other is imperfect - that markets 'fail' - is simply not sufficient to establish a case for government 'intervention'. (Brennan and Buchanan 1985, p. 130)

While the implications of this understanding are explored in later chapters, I emphasize for the moment that it is not at all clear that what animates the political process is an explicit accounting of a supraindividual 'socially desired' outcome. The maximand is clearly not a social welfare function. Rather, the political decision environment contemplates multiple objective functions and constraints - and frequently opaque decision processes. It is, in short, an environment characterized by information asymmetry and opportunistic behavior.

Whatever else is said, the liberal who seeks both to 'perfect' the market system and to promote 'social justice' should take account of the indeterminacy of social welfare theory, and of the imperfections of the political process.

NOTES

1. Because it seeks to promote the satisfaction of sanitized or non-external preferences, liberalism incorporates both a theory of the right (neutrality on what the good life is) and a theory of the good. It is in this sense that it is self-contradictory. See Section 3.1.
2. In fact, Dworkin acknowledges what he characterizes as 'the surface antagonism between rights and collective welfare' (1978, p. 367).
3. See also Paton (1964, pp. 20-21).
4. See also Scruton (1982, p. 72), O'Neill (1993, p. 184), Davis (1993, p. 211) and Rawls (1971, p. 563).
5. This objection applies with equal force to Dworkin's 'liberal theory of law' (Chapter 8).
6. *Inter alia*, this calls into question the educational establishment's 'psychological strategy'; a strategy which is, itself, grounded in the idea of an autonomous, transcendental, first-person self (S 2.3).
7. See also Tebbit (2000, p. 109), Almond (1993, pp. 265-6), Goodin (1993, p. 248) and Waldron (1995a, pp. 18-9).
8. The conflict between rights and utilitarianism has implications for the liberal theory of law. See Chapter 8.
9. It follows, *inter alia*, that the liberal theory of law cannot, logically, regard the law as a 'distributor of constitutional rights' (Scruton 2002, p. 73). For more on this see Chapter 8.
10. See Geoffrey Brennan (1995, p. 142) and Slesnick (1998, p. 2139).
11. See also Roth (2002, pp. 14-17).
12. For more on the neoclassical decision environment, see Furubotn and Richter (1991, pp. 11-12).

13. In the situation envisioned, a single-valued, consistently ordered social welfare function generates a family of social indifference curves. Granting this, a tangency of a social indifference curve and the efficiency frontier yields the unique, social welfare maximizing solution. The latter is understood to be the ethical equilibrium.
14. For more on this, see Demsetz (1996, pp. 4-5).
15. For critiques of economic man, see Thaler (2000), Knox (1999), Nelson (1995), Sen (1995), North (1994), Furubotn (1994), Tversky and Thaler (1990), Cox and Epstein (1989), Elster (1989).
16. See also Clarkson (1963, p. 99).
17. Recent experimental results involving equity, reciprocity and competition have been rationalized by appeal to evolutionary biology (Bolton and Ockenfels 2000). For more on this, see Robson (2001).
18. Heinrich (2000) presents evidence that 'economic decisions and economic reasoning may be heavily influenced by cultural differences - that is, by socially transmitted rules about how to behave in certain circumstances (economic or otherwise) that may vary from group to group as a consequence of different evolutionary trajectories' (p. 973). For experimental evidence on the effect of group attachment and social learning on economic behavior see Harbough and Krause (2000). For a survey of game theoretic and empirical efforts which suggest that cooperative behavior may be attributable to the development of social norms, see Ostrom (2000) and Fehr and Gächter (2000). Finally, for a sociological view of the endogeneity of preference structures, see Baron and Hannan (1994, p. 1117).
19. The possibility that learning may alter preference structures seems to have animated the Stigler and Becker effort (1977) to show that addiction, habit formation and other path-dependent phenomena are consistent with the stability of 'metapreferences'. For critical assessments of the Stigler and Becker approach, see Aaron (1994, p. 6), Pollak (1985, pp. 584-5), Furubotn (1994) and Roth (1998).
20. See Dowell, Goldfarb and Griffith (1998) for a model which includes moral concerns in utility functions and constraints.
21. See, for example, Hausman and McPherson (1993, p. 688), and Aaron (1994).
22. See also Rabin and Thaler (2001, p. 230).
23. Given the cognitive limitations which characterize the boundedly rational agent, Thaler (2000) predicts, *inter alia*, that '*Homo Economicus* will evolve into *Homo Sapiens*' (p. 140). For his part, Foster (2000) suggests that 'economic rationality is bounded not only by cognitive limitations but also by emotional considerations' (p.374).
24. For a contemporary expression of this view, see Buchanan (1991, p. 186).
25. See also Buchanan (1994b, pp. 82-3).
26. See Furubotn (1964, p. 22). See also Stigler (1987, pp. 136-8); Furubotn (1965); Roth (1974).
27. For formal representations of the choice of technique problem see Roth (1972; 1977).
28. For a characterization of the nature of decision costs see Furubotn and Richter (1997, pp. 31, 45 and 458).
29. For more on technical interaction, see Gort and Boddy (1965, p. 395) and Furubotn (1970, p. 22).
30. Cognitive limitations both militate against optimizing decisions and account for the disparity between agents' objective and subjectively perceived decision environments. This competence-difficulty gap has as one of its corollaries uncertainty about how to acquire and use information. In the face of complexity, agents 'systematically restrict the use and acquisition of information compared to that potentially available' (Heiner 1983, p. 564). See also Wilde, LeBaron and Israelsen (1985, p. 407).
31. See, for example, Frank (1996, p. 119) and Furubotn (1994).
32. For a discussion of the implications for utility functions of the disparate technical, aesthetic, property rights and ethical attributes of goods, see Roth (2002, p. 66).
33. See also Lipsey and Lancaster (1956, p. 13).
34. For more on the interpersonal utility comparison problem, see Roth (1999, pp. 48-51).

35. It is helpful in this context to recall that social welfare theory is predicated, in part, upon the existence not only of a 'benevolent despot', but of an 'omniscient being - the observing economist'. In this account, the omniscient observing economist 'possesses whatever information we may require about tastes, techniques, the future, and anything else' (Graaff 1957, p. 13). While Graaff clearly intended both construals as expository devices, it is at least arguable that these patently unrealistic generative assumptions (Roth 1998, Chapter 1), have metamorphosed into presumptive descriptions of reality (Roth 2002, Chapter 4).

36. Sen nevertheless asserts that 'The need to incorporate some "minimal liberties" on a priority basis can be incorporated in social choice formulations' (1995, p. 13). On the logic that rights cannot be consequence-detached Sen argues that consequential analysis can be employed in 'inverse form' to determine which rights to protect. While his idea is to embed rights protections in 'states of affairs', the difficulty is that rights and their correlative duties 'have a normative life of their own, with implications that are neither reducible to, nor traceable by, direct consideration of utility' (Lyons 1982, p. 133).

37. For more on this, see Brennan (1995, pp. 142-52).

5.   The First-Person Self: The Conservative's View

5.1   INTRODUCTION

To this point I have concentrated on an adumbration both of the liberal's constitutive political position (S 1.4) and its antecedents (S 1.3), and of the derivative positions which are regarded as instrumental to the achievement of the constitutive position (Chapter 2). Particular interest has centered on the Liberal Paradox (S 1.5), and upon the source of the conundrum, the liberal's misconstrual of the Kantian first-person self (S 3.2). We have seen moreover that, their protestations notwithstanding, liberals' insistence that government must be neutral with respect to what constitutes the good life is, itself, a theory of the good (S 3.1). Liberalism's natural rights and social justice construals fare no better (SS 3.3 and 3.4). Problems arise, both because liberalism deploys a truncated vision of the first-person self, and because utilitarianism is incommensurable with the Kantian idea which is 'the theoretical cornerstone of liberalism' (S 4.2). Equally important, its 'utilitarian connection' is irreconcilable with the moral force of the rights which liberalism seeks both to justify and to protect (S 4.3). Finally, liberalism's embrace of the economist's theory of the state (S 4.4) takes no account of the indeterminacy of the theory's fundamental theoretical constructs (SS 4.7 and 4.9), of the logical difficulties which encumber the path to first-best Paretian optima (S 4.8), or of the inability of the theory to accommodate any plausible understanding of justice (S 4.10).

Granting the logic of what has been said, fundamental logical, empirical and ontological problems attend the liberal enterprise. Something else is required. In what follows I shall argue that what is needed is a constitutive political position which, following Kant, deploys a first- *and* third-person conception of the self. What is required, in short, is a *conservative* conception of the self.

5.2   SOME PRELIMINARIES

Anthony Quinton (1995, pp. 244-5) has suggested that the 'main tradition of conservative thought derives from three central doctrines which are themselves connected'. According to this, 'traditionalism ... supports continuity in politics, the maintenance of existing institutions and practices and is suspicious of change, particularly of large and sudden change, and above all of violent and systematic revolutionary change'. For its part, political skepticism embodies the ideas that, on the one hand, the conservative is skeptical of 'abstract principles such as doctrines of universally applicable natural or human rights, ... utopias, [or] systematic proposals for comprehensive social transformation'. On the other hand, for the conservative, 'Political wisdom ... is embodied, first of all, in the inherited fabric of established laws and institutions'. Finally, 'Political skepticism ... rests on ... the conception of human beings and society as being organically or internally related'. In this view, 'Individual human beings are not fully formed, ... independently of the social institutions and practices within which they grow up. There is, therefore, no universal human nature'.

I do not disagree. Indeed, each of these ideas finds expression in Roger Scruton's important book, *The Meaning of Conservatism* (2002).[1] In Scruton's account, traditionalism, skepticism with respect to abstract political theory and organicism reduce to two principles that are 'so basic as to constitute axioms of conservative thinking: First, ... there is no general politics of conservatism. ... Second, ... conservatism engages with ... the motives, reasons, traditions and values of the society from which it draws its life' (p. 37).

Both axioms of conservative thought may, in turn, be traced to the conservative's conception of the self. Importantly, and in sharp contrast to the liberal's transcendental first-person self construal, the conservative's conception comports with Kant's 'two points of view' (S 3.2).

5.3   THE FIRST- *AND* THIRD-PERSON POINTS OF VIEW

Recall, first, that in the liberal's account, government must treat all persons with equal concern and respect, subject to the constraint that it must be neutral on what constitutes the 'good life' (S 1.4). As we have seen, this autonomy-based conception relies upon a truncated view of the Kantian, transcendental first-person self (S 3.2). While this is the foundation upon which the liberal's rights as trumps against external preferences construal is based (SS 1.4 and 3.3), it is also the source of the paradox of liberalism. Because the paradox is the subject of Section 1.5 it is sufficient for present purposes to note that the prevailing weakness of the liberal idea [is] surely this: that it reposes all politics and all morality in an idea of freedom while providing no philosophy of human nature which will tell us what freedom really is or why it matters. It isolates man from history, from culture, from all those unchosen aspects of himself which are in fact the preconditions of his subsequent autonomy. (Scruton 2002, p. 112)

The emphasis upon the self's spatio-temporal location or, what is the same thing, on the self's immersion in contingent circumstance, is consistent with Dworkin's characterization of the conservative's constitutive political position (S 1.4). More important, it is consistent with Kant's 'two points of view' (S 3.2). Reduced to its essentials, Kant insists that the transcendental first-person self cannot, by itself, provide a motive to respect the Moral Law. Agency and subjection to the strictures of the categorical imperative require immersion in contingent circumstance.[2]

In the conservative's account, the motive to respect the Kantian imperative to treat persons as ends rather than as means - to treat each person equally - cannot, as Kant acknowledged, be generated by the liberal's autonomous, transcendental, first-person self. It can, however, be cultivated:

consider what it is that leads people to see the world in terms of value, and so to develop the transcendental perspective which the liberal requires. People are born in a web of attachments; they are nurtured and protected by forces the operation of which they could neither consent to nor intend. Their very existence is burdened with a debt of love and gratitude, and it is in responding to that burden that they begin to recognize the power of 'ought'. This is not the abstract universal 'ought' of liberal theory - or, at least, not yet - but the immediate 'ought' of family attachments. It is the 'ought' of piety, which recognizes the unquestionable rightness of local, transitory and historically conditioned social bonds. (Scruton 2002, p. 192)

If the conservative's first- and third-person conception of the self comports with Kant's two points of view construal, it is also roughly congruent with Adam Smith's 'civilizing project' (S 1.3).[3] Whatever else is said, it is clear that conservatives embrace Kant's view that the transcendental first-person self has no motive either to act 'here and now' (Scruton 2002, p. 189), or to respect the imperative to treat persons as ends rather than as means. Yet the cultivation of the transcendental perspective, which the liberal values, requires precisely what he denies. For the liberal, the autonomous, transcendental self is morally sovereign, free to develop his own, subjective moral code. Indeed, as we have seen, the rights as trumps against external preferences construal is animated by an imperative to immunize the autonomous self from the intervention of others' altruistic, political and moralistic 'external preferences' (SS 1.4 and 3.3). It is clear, then, that the liberal enterprise has little in common with Kant's two points of view construal (S 3.2).

For the conservative, liberalism's peculiar autonomy construal is not simply a 'devious form of the Kantian Moral Law' (Scruton 2002, p. 73). The institutional skepticism which is a corollary of the single-minded pursuit of moral autonomy both denies the role and importance of the other dimensions of moral argument and appraisal and is too much concerned with private 'rights'.

5.4   ORDINARY CONSCIENCE

It has been suggested that 'the dominance of the liberal ideology is likely to be the cause not of freedom, but of license' (Scruton 2002, p. 68). While much can be said about this, the idea which animates this view is that liberalism's peculiar autonomy construal denies the functioning of 'ordinary conscience' (Scruton 1996, p. 126). In this view, the agent's action is both animated and constrained by four sources of moral reasoning and appraisal. To the question, 'How are moral conflicts resolved?' The conservative answers:

First, ... the moral law, when it speaks takes precedence. ... The essential function of morality, in creating a community founded in negotiation and consent, requires that rights and duties cannot be sacrificed to other interests.

But rights and duties can conflict. The result is a dilemma, and the distinguishing mark of a dilemma is that, while only one of two things can be done, you have a duty to do both. This duty is not cancelled by the dilemma; you merely have an excuse for not fulfilling it.

When the claims of right and duty have been satisfied, in so far as possible, the claims of virtue must be addressed. Even if the moral law neither forbids nor permits an action, there is still the question whether a virtuous person would perform it ... .

Finally, when all requirements of right and virtue have been met, we can respond to the call of sympathy; and here a kind of utilitarian thinking comes into play as the means to extend our sympathies to all whose interests are affected by our acts. Even so, the authority of this reasoning is not absolute: for sympathy may compete with piety. We rationalize our pieties by measuring them against our sympathies, and discipline our sympathies by testing them against the intuitions which stem from piety. (Scruton 1996, pp. 125-26)

While, as Scruton suggests, the ordering of the four sources of moral reasoning may be questioned and 'leaves much unresolved', the essential point is this: The Moral Law is both cultivated and supplemented by the ethic of virtue, by sympathy and by piety. Consistent with Kant's two points of view, the transcendental, autonomous first-person self can generate neither a motive to act nor a motive to respect the equal treatment imperative. The motive both to act, and to act in a manner consistent with the Moral Law requires immersion in contingent circumstance. It is precisely this brute fact which implicates the three sources of moral reasoning which, themselves, are reflective of the web of social attachments into which the individual is born.

In *The Theory of Moral Sentiments* Adam Smith endorses Dr. Francis Hutcheson's view that the principle of approbation and disapprobation - of approval or disapproval of character and conduct - flows both from reason and from 'immediate sense and feeling' ([1759] 1976 pp. 320-21).[4] This, it is clear, is the conservative's view:

> The moral being is not merely the rule-governed person who plays the game of rights and duties; he has a distinctive emotional character, which both fits him for the moral life and extends and modifies its edicts. He is a creature of extended sympathies, motivated by love, admiration, shame, and a host of other social emotions. (Scruton 1996, pp. 113-14)

In this view, virtues like courage, loyalty, decency, and a sense of justice and charity enjoy a reciprocal relationship with civil society. On the one hand, they are the 'qualities which preserve society'. On the other hand, they are 'shaped by material, spiritual and religious circumstances' (p. 114). For its part, sympathy - the 'thought which is peculiar to moral beings, involving a recognition of the distinction between self and other, and of the other as *feeling what I might have felt*' (p. 116) - is also reflective of the web of attachments which define the individual's social life. Finally, piety - the respect for sacred things - requires, for example, that we honor our parents and ancestors. But it also requires that we hesitate before seeking to change the established formal and informal institutional order (pp. 117-18). Yet piety is itself derivative of the 'allegiance which defines the condition of society, and which constitutes society as something greater than the "aggregate of individuals" that the liberal mind perceives' (Scruton 2002, p. 24). In this account, the family bond is central to the formation of allegiance and, *pari passu*, to the 'residue of respect or piety which grows from that, ripe for transference to whatever might present itself as a fitting social object' (p. 25).

If the conservative's ordinary conscience conception is consistent with Kant's two points of view, it is irreconcilable with the liberal's transcendental, autonomous self construal. For the conservative, the first-person self is not a moral being. Absent a third-person perspective, the transcendental, autonomous self has neither a motive to act nor a motive to respect the moral law. For the liberal - despite the Kantian roots of his conception - the transcendental, autonomous moral being is entitled both to ask 'Why should I do that?' (Scruton 2002, p. 186) and to insist that he has natural rights against others' intrusive altruistic, political and moralistic external preferences. For the conservative, the former is corrosive of the conditions which nurture the Moral Law, while the latter cannot be reconciled with Kant's two points of view (S 3.3).

5.5 THE CONSERVATIVE'S CONSTITUTIVE POSITION

If the transcendental, autonomous first-person self is the theoretical cornerstone of liberalism, the Kantian two-person point of view is the foundation upon which the conservative's constitutive position is built.

Given this predicate, certain corollaries follow. First, the conservative rejects the liberal's natural rights as non-absolute trumps against external preferences construal. For the conservative, rights cannot be construed to be 'possessed antecedently to all specific claims within an organized society' (MacDonald [1947-1948] 1995, p. 21).[5] Insofar as external preferences subsume political, altruistic and moralistic preferences or values, 'any area of social life which is vital either to the strength of the social bond, or to the social image of its participants, will be one into which the law may legitimately intrude' (Scruton 2002, p. 73). While this idea is more fully developed in Chapter 8, the essential idea is that this 'collusion between social values and norms' (p. 132) is antithetical to the moral pluralism to which the liberal's transcendental first-person perspective gives rise (S 2.2).[6] It is clear, then, that the tolerance imperative which is central to the liberal's constitutive position (S 1.6) is incommensurable with the conservative's view. In short, the conservative rejects the notion that the law 'cannot legitimately infringe the "natural" right of citizens to do as they please' (p. 66). Thus, while Dworkin, quite plausibly, rejects the view that 'Liberals tend relatively to favor equality more and liberty less than conservatives do' (1985, pp. 188-9), the conservative insists that the liberal's transcendental 'natural' rights against the state project 'remove(s) from the law the image of a particular social arrangement'. In this view,

> The civil society is confirmed in the institutions of the state; law, as the will of the state, is therefore the concrete reality of civil life. To the extent that, one by one, customs, manners, morals, education, labour and the rest are 'liberated' from its jurisdiction, so too does the sense of their social validity suffer a decline, as citizens find the gulf widening between their customs and their form of life, and the law which supposedly protects them. (Scruton 2002, pp. 74-5)

It is the idea which informs the second corollary of the conservative's Kantian two-person point of view. Whereas 'it has been the business of liberalism to prise state and society apart' (p. 62),

> Conservatives are recognizable as political animals partly by their respect for constitution (for the state as 'given'), and by their reluctance to effect any complete separation - either in theory or in practice - between state and civil society ... .

> Conservatives see the constitution as the inherited principle of the state, and the state in its turn not just as the guardian but also as the expression of a social entity. (p. 40)

For the conservative, the constitution is not founded in 'natural rights'. But it 'and the institutions which sustain it, will always be at the heart of [his] thinking' (p. 25). Yet the institutions which both animate and sustain the constitution are the customs, traditions, precedents and law which engender a sense of 'nationhood' and allegiance'.[7] In this account, individuals

> must see themselves as the inheritors, not the creators of the order in which they participate, so that they may derive from it (from the picture of its 'objectivity') the conceptions and values which determine self-identity. They will see their extension in time from birth to death as taking on significance from civil stability: their world was not born with them, nor does it die when they depart from it. (p. 60)

'Allegiance', in this account, 'constitutes society as something greater than the "aggregate of individuals" that the liberal mind perceives'. The essential idea is that individuals *do* 'exist and act as autonomous beings', but they do so 'only because they can first identify themselves as something greater - as members of a society, group, class, state or nation'. Granting this 'For many people, the bond of allegiance has immediate authority, while the call to individuality is unheard' (p. 24).

None of this suggests that the conservative denies the individual's autonomy. Indeed, 'it is the individual's responsibility to win whatever freedom of speech, conscience and assembly he may' (p. 8). Yet 'if individuality threatens allegiance - as it must do in a society where individuality seeks to realize itself in opposition to the institutions from which it grows - then the civil order is threatened too' (p. 25).[8]

If customs, traditions, precedents and law engender both a sense of nationhood and allegiance, it is the *constitution* - itself informed by these informal and formal institutions (p. 60) - which underwrite the *legitimate power* or *authority* of government. In the conservative view,

> the constitution consists in those rules and customs through which people engage in the exercise of power: it is what guides, limits and authorizes power, and thus manifests itself primarily through law, through the 'style' of law, and through the position of the citizen as defined by law. It may change and develop in accordance with its own inner logic - the logic of precedent, practice and judicial abstraction. The conservative instinct is not to prevent that change - since it is the vital motion of the state - but to guard the essence which survives it, and which enables us to say that its various stages are stages in the life of one body politic. And the constitutional essence guards in its turn the social essence. Here then, is the conservative cause in politics. (p. 45)

Now, as has been emphasized, the *legitimacy* of government derives from the allegiance of the governed. That said, 'the legitimacy of government cannot be conferred merely by democratic choice' (p. 46). Stated differently, 'democracy' is not necessary and sufficient to confer legitimacy upon government. In fact, legitimacy is conferred by established usage; by the customs, traditions and other informal and formal institutions which, themselves, both inform and sustain the constitution. It follows that other forms of government may gain allegiance and, through this, the authority to exercise legitimate power or authority.

That said, in what follows I shall assume that post-constitutional or day-to-day conflictual politics unfolds in the context of a constitutional democracy. Recall first that, in principle, 'a constitutional democracy can be arranged so as to satisfy the principle of [equal political] participation' (Rawls 1971, p. 222).[9] Animated as he is by the Kantian first-person perspective, Rawls suggests that 'the constitutional process should preserve the equal representation of the [Kantian] original position to the degree that is practicable' (p. 222). In contrast, for the conservative, equal political participation both respects the moral equivalence of persons and gives voice to the altruistic, political and moralistic external preferences which characterize contingent circumstance.

For the conservative, then, representative democracy is reconcilable with the Kantian first- and third-person perspectives.[10] Yet, if representative - hereafter, majoritarian - democracy can give expression to Kant's two points of view, it must be constrained. On the one hand, 'As it operates, [because] postconstitutional politics is majoritarian, [it is], naturally, discriminatory to the extent that participants promote separable interests' (Buchanan and Congleton 1998, p. 12).[11] This 'rent seeking' activity is both inherently discriminatory and wasteful of resources. On the other hand, 'cycling' is a characteristic of majoritarian democracy (Arrow 1951; Black 1958). In effect, majority coalitions may extract in-period benefits from, and/or impose costs upon, members of the extant minority. Yet this in-period discrimination may be accepted on the 'implicit understanding [that] dominant groups rotate sequentially over electoral periods' (Buchanan and Congleton 1998, pp. 19-20). Whatever else is said, the 'cycling' of discriminatory treatment may properly be characterized as the 'politics of taking' (p. 19). Relatedly, the politics of taking contemplates inter-generational discrimination:

> however fair and free, [the democratic process] will always give precedence to the needs and desires of those who are choosing now regardless of the needs and desires of those who are not yet with us, or those who are already dead. (Scruton 2002, p. 47)

Given these defects of 'untrammeled democracy' (p. 50), the conservative's constitutive position envisions procedural limitations on the democratic process (p. 48).[12] Of central importance is what Buchanan and Congleton (1998) have characterized as a generality or impartiality constraint. While majoritarian agreement cannot, on conservative logic, contemplate any 'constitutionally protected sphere of activity into which politics cannot legitimately enter' (p. 19), this much can be said *a priori*: A constitutional generality constraint is not consequentialist. The procedural or institutional imperative is the minimization of intra- and intergenerational discrimination. It follows, *inter alia*, that interest centers on *political* rather than economic efficiency or 'first-best Paretian optimality'. While more will be said of this in Chapter 6, political efficiency is understood to 'describe the efficacy of differing institutions in reducing or eliminating the incentives for [political] participants to invest resources in rent seeking aimed to secure discriminatory advantage through majoritarian exploitation' (Buchanan and Congleton 1998, p. 40). It follows that

> the legitimacy of basic constitutional principles is judged not against some predefined 'ideal system' but in terms of the process from which these principles emerge. The normative focus is on the characteristics of the process of constitutional choice, not on characteristics of choice-outcomes as such. Furthermore, ... a 'good' or 'proper' process is defined as one that assures *fairness* or *impartiality* in the rules that emerge. (Buchanan 1991, p. 59)

The rejection of outcomes-based evaluation is clearly reflective of the true Kantian perspective (S 4.2). This, and the disinclination to invoke a 'predefined "ideal system"' is descriptive of the conservative's constitutive political position:

> It is the mark of rational intercourse that aims are not all predetermined, that some ends - perhaps the most important ends - remain to be discovered rather than imposed. And in the life of society they are discovered not by the perusal of utopian treatises, but, primarily, through participation. ... One might say that, for the conservative, political ends make sense in conduct, but for the most part resist translation into recipes. (Scruton 2002, p. 13)

If, for the conservative, conflictual or day-to-day politics has no 'ruling purpose', he insists that the constitution be informed by ordinary conscience and all that it implies (S 5.4). It is central to this project, then, that intra- and intergenerational discrimination be constitutionally prohibited. It is in this sense that the conservative's approach comports with that of the constitutional political economist:

> Normatively, the task of the constitutional political economist is to assist individuals, as citizens who ultimately control their own social order, in their continuing search for those rules of the political game that will best serve their purposes, whatever they may be. (Buchanan 1987, p. 250)

To this, the conservative would add that the constitution must provide the 'framework within which individuals can pursue their ambitions in ways that contribute to social harmony' (Scruton 2002, p. 176). In this account, 'People have the idea of legitimacy. ... and a society is not happy in which people cannot see that legitimacy enacted, in which they see only state coercion, and only established power' (p. 19). Given the conservative's commitment to Kant's two points of view (S. 3.2), the operation of ordinary conscience (S 5.4) is understood to be a *sine qua non* both for social harmony and the legitimate power or authority of government. It is precisely this idea which animates the constitutional generality or impartiality imperative - and the work of the constitutional political economist.

Granting all of this, two questions remain: First, is a constitutional generality constraint *possible*? Second, how is the constitution to be defended?

I stipulate, first, that a veil of ignorance-situated agreement on a generality of impartiality constraint is not, by definition, possible at the postconstitutional or conflictual politics stage. That said, citizen-agents may be moved by ordinary conscience to institutionalize a constitutionally mandated generality constraint. Yet the 'publicness' of constitutional provisions - and of the rule of law - must be acknowledged. In effect, ' the structure of law ... represents social or public capital stock, the yield from which accrues through a sequence of time periods' (Buchanan [1975] 2000, p. 156). Given the publicness and the potential durability of *any* constitutional change, two problems must be faced. On the one hand, the present value of the net expected benefits to an idealized person who expects to live forever will exceed that of the agent whose planning horizon is finite (pp. 157-8). On the other hand, when the expected benefits of constitutional rule changes accrue publicly, the question arises, 'Who are to take upon themselves the personal burden of designing provisional proposals for basic changes in the rules?' (Brennan and Buchanan [1985] 2000, p. 16). Reduced to its essentials, the lack of correspondence between ideal and actual planning horizons may, when added to the 'free rider' problem, militate against a constitutional generality constraint.

In the face of these difficulties - and given the moral exigency, instrumental importance, and publicness of a generality constraint - it seems clear that constitutional dialogue must be encouraged (Buchanan [1989] 1999, p. 369). The dialogue may, in turn, be facilitated by what James Buchanan has called 'preaching' (1991, p. 186; 1994b, p. 80; 1994a). According to Buchanan, the citizen-agent must be made to understand that he has an 'ethical responsibility of full and informed participation in a continuing constitutional convention' ([1989] 1999, p. 372). This, it should be noted, comports with Rawls' duty of justice construal:

From the standpoint of justice as [impartiality], a fundamental natural duty is the duty of justice. This duty requires us to support and to comply with just institutions that exist and apply to us. It also constrains us to further just arrangements not yet established, at least when this can be done without too much cost to ourselves. (1971, p. 115)[13]

There remains, then, the question of how, from the conservative's perspective, a constitution is to be defended. Recall, first, that the liberal's constitutive political position regards rights as non-absolute trumps against external preferences (SS 1.4 and 3.3), and the economist's theory of the state - social welfare theory - as instrumental both to the 'perfectibility' of the market system and the achievement of 'social justice' (S 3.4). While the logical, empirical and ontological problems with the liberal's constitutive position need not be reprised here, it is clear that the liberal seeks 'to remake the nation through statute, and to substitute statute wherever possible for common law, even in defiance of natural justice' (Scruton 2002, p. 57). Because the liberal 'sees the state [both] as a means to the end of individual freedom' (p. 38) and as a means to 'perfect' the market system, he 'seeks statutes that are immune from judicial qualification'. Moreover, he seeks statutes which 'come in fact succession, forbidding time to the community in which to take stock of change'. Granting this, 'in the fever of fomented change, the [independent] judiciary must act as a conservative force. For judges seek to align the decrees of [the legislative body] with an established legal system, and hence (indirectly) with institutions that find protection under the existing body of law' (p. 58). From this perspective,

> Those who suspect the judiciary, under common-law jurisdictions, of being a conservative force, are surely right. A judge acting under the discipline of [common] law can do no other than respect the social arrangement that is expressed in law. In doing justice he removes resentment and so indirectly restores some part of the *status quo*. (p. 58)

It is in this sense that an *independent* judiciary must serve to protect citizens 'from the state's encroachments' (p. 175).[14]

Finally, having once again invoked the idea of the liberal's embrace of the economist's theory of the state it is important to emphasize that social welfare theory has no place in the conservative's constitutive position. On the one hand, while the theory's fundamental constructs - the efficiency frontier and the social welfare function - are indeterminate (SS 4.7 and 4.9), the first and second fundamental welfare theorems are deployed to 'justify' both government market interventions and redistribution schemes. In effect, the theory has facilitated the discriminatory rent seeking which the conservative abhors. On the other hand, the theory can accommodate neither the moral force of rights (S 4.3), nor any plausible theory of justice (S 4.10). Finally, because it is consequentialist, its focus, in liberal hands, is the promotion of 'social justice' - a concept which cannot be reconciled with Kant's two-person point of view (S 3.4).

NOTES

1. See, for example, Scruton (2002, pp. 30-36, 18-27 and 27-9).
2. See, expecially Kant ([1785] 1988, pp. 87-8) and the discussion in Section 3.2.
3. See, especially Smith ([1759] 1976, pp. 163 and 200). The implications for economics of an explicit accounting of the first- and third-person perspectives and, relatedly, of Smith's civilizing project are developed in Chapter 7.
4. For more on Smith's views on the social cultivation of moral sentiments see Section 1.3.
5. See Section 3.3.
6. This conception comports, I suggest, with Kant's view that all political issues are moral issues (Kersting 1992, p. 343).
7. See Scruton (2002, p. 174 and pp. 25-7).
8. It should be clear that this idea - along with the conservative's rejection of the liberal's transcendental autonomous self construal - informs the conservative's opposition both to the rights as trumps against external preferences construal and the liberal's 'reforming spirit'.
9. For a discussion of the meaning, extent and worth of equal political participation, see Rawls (1971, pp. 223-8).
10. Moreover, while in a representative democracy 'There is no known method for securing "rule by the best" ... . What is valuable in democracy is that such mistakes can be corrected. The discovery that we have voted for the wrong people leads eventually to their ejection from office' (Scruton 2002, p. 50).
11. At the most rudimentary level, prospective beneficiaries of government spending and tax policies appreciate that, whereas the benefits will be concentrated, the costs of such initiatives will be widely dispersed. Interestingly, this concentrated benefit-dispersed cost phenomenon was described at the end of the nineteenth century by Vilfredo Pareto (1896). See also Buchanan (1986, pp. 254-5).
12. See also Scruton (2002, p. 53).
13. It is, of course, possible to argue that, immersed in contingent circumstance, the citizen-agent may, out of *self-interest*, endorse a generality constraint. The essential idea is that, if majoritarian cycling is recognized, 'it may become rational for the members of the ruling majority coalition to support the constitutional change that will incorporate the generality principle, even in the understanding that adoption of such a rule will mean foregoing current period gains from discriminatory exploitation' (Buchanan and Congleton 1998, p. 57). See also Buchanan and Tullock (1962, p. 96).
14. It should be clear that what is envisioned here is the familiar division of government powers among the executive, the legislature, and the judiciary.

6.   Derivative Political Positions

6.1   ORDINARY CONSCIENCE, CIVIL SOCIETY AND FREEDOM

The tolerance imperative (S 1.6) is animated by liberalism's insistence that the transcendental, autonomous self must be given 'as much moral and political space ... as is compatible with the demands of social life' (Scruton 2002, p. 182). As we have seen, the normative relativism to which the imperative naturally gives rise (S 2.2) informs the educational establishment's 'psychological strategy' (S 2.3). Grounded as it is in the ethical neutrality of secular psychology, the strategy assumes that the autonomous, first-person self is 'perfectible'. Freed from the 'despotism of custom', tradition and the 'web of attachments' into which he is born, the autonomous self is presumed to 'possess an innate capacity for moral goodness; character resides within each of us, largely independent of the relationships we have or the communities into which we are born. These endowments only need to be coaxed out and developed within the personality' (Hunter 2000, p. 10). If, as Tappan and Brown suggest, 'This vision ... seeks to use education ... to enable each student to resist and overcome social and cultural repression, and hence to authorize his or her own moral voice' (1989, p. 24), it also give rise to what Hunter has called the 'paradox of inclusion'. Reduced to its essentials, there is 'tension between accommodating diversity in public life and establishing a working agreement in our moral life' (2000, p. 9).

Given his commitment to the Kantian two-person self (S 3.2) and the associated ordinary conscience construal (S 5.4) the conservative rejects the educational establishment's psychological strategy (S 2.4). On the one hand, the strategy 'exclude[s] the possibility of commitments that go beyond subjective choices or obligations that are antecedent to personal choice' (Hunter 2000, p. 187). On the other hand, the institutional skepticism to which the strategy gives rise is corrosive of the conditions which make civil society and freedom *possible*.

Writing in 1976 the Nobel laureate economist, James Buchanan, adumbrated the implications of 'individually determined norms of obedience':

Despite the Great Depression, the men of 1935 honored politics and politicans, and patriotism remained extant as a major motive force. There was widespread respect for 'law' as such, and rare indeed were those who felt themselves morally capable of choosing individually determined norms of obedience.

Alongside these disintegrating institutions, which tended to establish and to maintain order and stability in society, with the predictable effects of such disintegration on individual adherence to traditional moral norms, the school must be placed. Within the context of strong and stable institutions of family, church, and state, the school can appropriately combine a rational transmission of moral values with a critical and searching reexamination of these values. As the offsets are weakened, however, and as the internal mix within the school changes toward criticism and away from transmitting value, this institution becomes one of disorder and instability in modern society. (1979, p. 215)

To this I would add that, for the conservative, 'moral neutrality' both denies the operation of ordinary conscience and misconstrues the Kantian equal treatment imperative. In the first instance, it denies the role and importance - both for the individual *and* for society - of the motivating and constraining force of the ethic of virtue, of sympathy, and of piety. In the second instance it presumes, Kant's two points of view and Adam Smith's 'civilizing project' (S 1.3) notwithstanding, that the individual is morally sovereign. Taken together, the denial and the misconstrual are both the source of the Paradox of Liberalism (S 1.5) and the genesis of all manner of 'equality'-animated casuistries. I emphasize, in particular, the 'diversity' imperative (S 2.5). While the argument need not be reprised here, diversity in the sense of affirmative action and multiculturalism is, in the liberal's account, instrumental to the achievement of a 'more equal society'. For the conservative, the juxtaposition of the liberal's autonomous, transcendental first-person self and an imperative to derive one's 'identity' from group attachment is both incongruous and incommensurable with the *Kantian* imperative to treat the *individual* as end rather than as means. Equally important, the liberal's diversity project is a reflection of his 'reforming spirit', a propensity which 'constitutes a threat, not only to the state, but also to society'. In the conservative's view, 'The spirit of reform has been too much concerned with private "rights", and not enough concerned with the public order and private duties that make [rights] possible' (Scruton 2002, p. 175).

If the conservative rejects the liberal's rights as trumps against external preferences construal, he also recognizes that the moral force of legally sanctioned rights is eroded both by the metastasization of asserted 'natural rights', and by autonomy-based institutional skepticism. While it is true that the conservative's derivative political positions are, and must be, responsive to the vagaries of contingent circumstance, this much can be said *a priori*: The conservative rejects the caprice of 'tolerance', of 'diversity', and of 'self-realization'. Each, in its own way, is corrosive of the sense of duty which makes respect for legally sanctioned rights possible. Neither rights specification nor respect for rights' correlative duties can emanate from the transcendental, autonomous self. Rights and, *pari passu*, the distribution of freedom, are the reflection of a civil society informed by ordinary conscience; by the interaction of the Moral Law, the ethic of virtue, sympathy and piety. It is, in short, the Kantian two-person point of view which informs the conservative's derivative political positions.

6.2   THE PROCEDURAL IMPERATIVES

Without further justificatory argument, I assert that, given their Kantian roots, the conservative's constitutive and derivative political positions are not, and cannot be, consequentialist.[1] Because the conservative does not interpret the right as maximizing the good,[2] he seeks neither to maximize 'social welfare' (S 4.5) nor to promote 'social justice' (S 3.4). Rather, the imperative is procedural. I emphasize, first, that the moral equivalence of persons demands that legally sanctioned rights - rights which cannot be antecedent to civil society - be respected (SS 3.3 and 5.5). While the character and content of rights - and of rights restrictions - cannot be established *a priori* this much can be said: The extant and emergent rights structure is not the province of the transcendental, autonomous self. Rather, it reflects the fundamental values or external political, altruistic and moralistic preferences of society. Insofar as ordinary conscience (S 5.4) 'leads people to see the world in terms of value, and so to develop the [true Kantian] first-person perspective' (Scruton 2002, p. 12), legal rights will come, also, to reflect the Moral Law. In short, both the rights structure and, equally important, the rights restrictions embraced by civil society must reflect Kant's two points of view (S 3.2). Absent this perspective, neither legally sanctioned rights nor rights restrictions can have moral force. Stated differently, recognition and acceptance of the duty to respect such rights is incommensurable with the institutional skepticism that is characteristic of the liberal's transcendental first-person self (SS 1.4 and 3.4).

If the Kantian two-person point of view requires that legally sanctioned rights be respected, it also demands that the constitutional rules which constrain postconstitutional conflictual politics be consonant with the emergence of just, in the sense of impartial, laws. This imperative is both a corollary of the moral equivalence of persons and a *sine qua non* for the exercise of government's *legitimate power* or *authority* (S 5.5). Granting this, and given the discriminatory rent seeking and majoritarian cycling which characterize it, postconstitutional politics must be procedurally constrained. What is required, in short, is a constitutional generality or impartiality constraint (Buchanan and Congleton 1998, p. 7). Here, the desideratum is neither the promotion of social justice nor the achievement of first-best Paretian or efficient outcomes. Rather, it is the reduction or elimination of 'incentives for participants [in postconstitutional politics] to invest resources in rent seeking aimed to secure discriminatory advantage through majoritarian exploitation' (p. 40). It is in this sense that political efficiency is consistent with the Moral Law and with natural justice (S 3.4).

Finally, I emphasize, again, that the pursuit of 'good ends' is incommensurable with Kantian ethics and, *pari passu*, with the conservative's constitutive political position. For the conservative, 'some ends - perhaps the most important ends - remain to be discovered rather than imposed. And in the life of society they are discovered not by the perusal of utopian treatises, but, primarily through participation' (Scruton 2002, p. 13). While this indeterminacy of 'ends' may be troublesome to some, it is a logical consequence of the conservative's, and of the constitutional political economist's, two-person Kantian perspective.[3] Thus, if the liberal may imagine a constitutional constraint which instructs legislators 'to disregard the external preferences of their constituents' (Dworkin 1985, p. 197), the conservative - and the constitutional political economist - envision no such constraint. Rather, voters' political, altruistic and moralistic values are understood to 'count'. Granting this, *whatever* policies are endorsed, intra - and intergenerational discrimination must be constitutionally constrained.

6.3   CONFLICTUAL POLITICS, RENT SEEKING AND THE CONSTITUTION

The moral equivalence of persons, an idea drawn from Kantian moral philosophy, has an analogue in political philosophy. The principle of equal participation

> requires that all citizens are to have an equal right to take part in, and to determine the outcome of, the constitutional process that establishes the laws with which they are to

comply. Justice as [impartiality] begins with the idea that where common principles are necessary and to everyone's advantage, they are to be worked out from the viewpoint of a suitably defined initial situation of equality in which each person is fairly represented. The principle of participation transfers this notion from the original position to the constitution as the highest-order system of social rules for making rules. (Rawls 1971, pp. 221-2)[4]

As we have seen (S 5.5), a constitutional democracy can, in principle, be arranged so as to satisfy the principle of equal political participation. *Inter alia*, this requires that the constitution 'be framed so that of all feasible just arrangements, it is the one more likely than any other to result in a just and effective system of legislation' (Rawls 1971, p. 221). In short, given the moral equivalence of persons, the constitution must provide rules for conflictual, postconstitutional politics which are consonant with the emergence of just or impartial legislation.

The substantive aims or values that law ought to promote - its 'external morality' - find expression in these ideas (Ten 1995, p. 397). In this account, 'the conception of formal justice, the regular and impartial administration of public rules, becomes the rule of law when applied to the legal system' (Rawls 1971, p. 235). From the perspective of the constitutional political economist, this impartiality or generality principle should be extended to politics (Buchanan and Congleton 1998, p. 7).

How, then, might a constitutional democracy be arranged so as to promote equal political participation and respect the external morality of law? At the constitutional stage, the principle of equal participation *means* that each vote has approximately the same weight, that members of the legislature, with one vote each, represent the same number of electors, and that all citizens have equal access to public office (Rawls 1971, p. 223). The *extent* of equal participation is 'the degree to which the procedure of (bare) majority rule is restricted by the mechanisms of constitution' (p. 228). Thus majorities have 'final authority' on 'devices which serve to limit the scope of majority rule', subject to the constraint that 'limits on the extent of the principle of [equal] participation [must] fall equally upon everyone' (p. 228).[5] Finally, and of particular importance to post-constitutional politics, the *worth* or value of equal political participation requires that the constitution 'underwrite a fair opportunity to take part in and to influence the political process' (p. 224). *Inter alia*, this requires that all citizens 'should have the means to be informed about political issues' (p. 225). The imperative, in short, is to prevent the pleadings of the 'more advantaged social and economic interests' from receiving 'excessive attention' (p. 226).[6]

If the external morality of law is grounded in the Moral Law, its internal morality is captured by 'the precepts of justice associated with the rule of law'. The precepts, in turn, 'are those that would be followed by any system of rules which perfectly embodied the idea of a legal system' (Rawls 1971, p. 236).

There are, in Lon Fuller's account (1971), eight such precepts or principles: (1) the law should be general in the sense that it lays down general standards of conduct; (2) laws should be promulgated or made known to those to whom they apply; (3) laws should be prospective rather than retroactive; (4) laws should be clear; (5) laws should not be contradictory; (6) laws should not demand the impossible; (7) laws should not be changed frequently; and (8) laws should require a congruence between official action and the relevant statutes.

The eight principles of internal morality of law are roughly congruent with Rawls' account (1971, pp. 236-9). We need only to add that 'there are those precepts defining the notion of natural justice. These are guidelines intended to preserve the integrity of the judicial process'.[7]

Whatever else is said, the essential point is that the Moral Law implies a set of institutional imperatives. On the one hand, the external morality of law demands that each person have a fair opportunity to take part in and to influence the political process, and that elected representatives pass just, in the sense of impartial, legislation. On the other hand, the internal morality of law demands that laws be general, be made known, be prospective, and be clear and not contradictory. In addition, laws must not demand the impossible, they must not be changed frequently, and they should require that official action be congruent with the law. These ideas inform the balance of Chapter 6, and the discussion in Chapter 8.

6.4   THE LEGISLATIVE PROCESS

I stipulate, first, that voters, like all agents, are boundedly rational (S 4.6). Granting this, cognitive limitations on the reception, storage, retrieval and processing of information impel voters to partition interrelated issues. It follows, therefore, that elected representatives have wide discretion over the character and content of legislative actions (Kuran 1991, pp. 242 and 252-3). Thus, for example, a tariff on 'illegally subsidized' airframes may be regarded by voters as both 'fair' and costless. Yet, insofar as it results in an increase in the price of domestically produced commercial jets and, ultimately, in airfares, the tariff is not costless. Elected representatives may, nevertheless, secure support for intendedly discriminatory trade restraints based upon voters' failure to appreciate the implications of the market intervention. Under the circumstances envisioned, voter 'oversight' is clearly unavailing.

The essential point is that voters' propensity to partition issues renders them vulnerable to 'special interest' rent seeking. Yet, if the root cause of the problem is voters' bounded rationality, its correlatives, information asymmetry, opportunism and high *ex ante* and *ex post* monitoring costs compound the problem (Williamson 1985). So, too, does institutional 'logrolling'.

It is well known that lawmakers carrying special interest legislation can 'rarely succeed on their own'. Problems arise because 'for any measure or set of measures devised through negotiation and exchange, there exists another measure that will command a majority against it'. In effect, 'No [legislative initiative benefitting one interest] is invulnerable to an alternative proposal ... no legislative exchange in an unstructured legislature is self-enforcing' (Weingast 1991, p. 263).

The United States Congress has sought, like other legislative bodies, to resolve the problem by creating some 200 committees and subcommittees, each of which is intended to have jurisdiction over a discrete subset of policy 'issues' (Ornstein, Mann and Malbin 2000, Table 4-2). While jurisdictional issues inevitably arise, each committee or subcommittee has 'gate keeping power' over the initiation and, in some instances, the 'flow' of legislation.[8] Significantly and, it must be said, predictably, because of their specialized institutional knowledge, or human capital specificity,[9] committee members have a comparative 'knowledge' advantage: Committee members both initiate legislation and shape the information which flows to other Members of Congress. Yet, if the Committee structure provides venues for the drafting or 'mark up' of disparate 'bills', it does not, by itself, resolve the logrolling problem: The question remains, How does a committee command the support of a majority when its legislation comes before the House or the Senate?

The solution is bundling legislation. Characteristically, provisions benefitting narrow special interests or targeted congressional districts are bundled together in 'omnibus' bills whose size and arcane language make effective monitoring a virtual impossibility. Indeed, if omnibus bills solve the logrolling problem, the *ex ante* and *ex post* monitoring costs effectively disenfranchise both voters *and* Members of Congress. On the one hand, because reneging on agreements to support each others' projects would doom the entire bill, individual legislators have an incentive to support the entire bill. On the other hand, neither the individual Member nor his/her staff can, in the typical rush of legislative events, be expected to have *read*, let alone comprehended, the content and implications of omnibus bills.[10]

It is tautological that omnibus tax, appropriations, spending or other bills are incommensurable with the external and internal morality of the law. Omnibus bills deny the voter both a 'fair opportunity to take part in and to influence the political process' (Rawls 1971, p. 224), and 'the means to be informed about political issues' (p. 225). Moreover, it is clear that Members of Congress cannot plausibly be construed to be seeking to pass just, in the sense of impartial, legislation.

Simply stated, omnibus bills deny voters their right, as morally equivalent 'equal citizens' to equal political participation. It follows, *mutatis mutandis*, that omnibus bills violate the external morality of law. The same is true, of course, of the law's internal morality. *Inter alia*, such bills clearly violate the precept that laws should be made known to those to whom they apply (S 6.3). It is in any case apparent that the concentrated benefit-dispersed cost calculus finds amplified expression in omnibus bills: If the concentrated beneficiaries can plausibly be assumed to have exhaustive knowledge of bill provisions which benefit them, those who bear the dispersed costs are likely, frequently, to be unaware of the provisions' *existence*.

Given that rent seeking is endemic to postconstitutional politics, and given that 'no Congress can bind a succeeding Congress by a simple statute' (Hatch 1981, p. 42), a statutory solution is unavailing. It seems clear that, if the moral equivalence of persons and their right to equal political participation are to be respected, a *constitutional* remedy is required. While a constitutional generality or impartiality constraint cannot, in the face of path-dependent contingent circumstance, contemplate either an *a priori* limit on the number of congressional committees or a prohibition against logrolling, it can require that all legislation respect the external and internal morality of law. What is required is a constitutional prohibition against omnibus or bundling legislation.[11]

It might, of course, be objected that a constitutional prohibition of omnibus legislation would 'slow the legislative process'. To this, the conservative response is unambiguous: Good! *Inter alia*, this would both reduce the burden placed upon the independent judiciary and enhance the probability of emergence of just, in the sense of impartial, legislation.

Finally, it must be acknowledged that the right to equal political participation carries with it a correlative duty. In the instant case, justice as impartiality and, *pari passu*, the right to equal political participation, implies a 'duty of justice'. As we have seen (S 5.5), the duty 'requires us to comply with just institutions that exist and apply to us. It also constrains us to further just arrangements not yet established, at least when this can be done without too much cost to ourselves' (Rawls 1971, p. 115).[12] In effect, citizens have a duty both to engage in constitutional discourse and to promote the constitutionalization of a generality constraint, *inter alia*, on the legislative process. Then, in the postconstitutional or conflictual politics stage, the duty of justice implies an obligation actively to participate in the political process generally and, in particular, to monitor the legislative process.

While evidence suggests that the duty of justice may not be respected,[13] this much is clear: For the conservative, the right to equal political participation, the political inefficiency of postconstitutional majoritarian politics, and the bounded rationality of citizens argue for a constitutional generality constraint on the legislative process. The constraint, in turn, must contemplate a prohibition against omnibus legislation.

6.5 ON- AND OFF-BUDGET ACTIVITY

United States budget law distinguishes between on- and off-budget activity. Social Security and the Postal Service are 'off-budget', with 'on-budget' understood to mean 'the transactions of all Federal Government entities except those excluded from the budget totals by law' (Office of Management and Budget, *Analytical Perspectives*, 2003, pp. 474-5).

I emphasize first that much attention has centered on the so-called Unified Budget. The latter, understood to be 'the presentation of the Federal budget in which revenues from all sources and outlays to all activities are consolidated',[14] aggregates on- and off-budget revenues and outlays. Significantly, during the period 1946 to 2002 the federal government's on-budget accounts have been in deficit in all but eight years. In sharp contrast, the off-budget accounts - essentially Social Security payroll tax receipts net of Social Security disbursements - have been in surplus in all but thirteen years (Office of Management and Budget, *Historical Tables*, 2003, pp. 21-2). Considered *in vacuo* these facts are both interesting and important. Yet it is of particular interest that the off-budget surpluses have generally been used to finance on-budget outlays. It seems clear that the 'representative' taxpayer is unaware of this particular casuistry.[15]

That said, the issue of immediate concern is the temporal character of government borrowing. The essential point is that, whether on- or off-budget, the purpose of borrowing 'is to implement the temporal transposition of value - to postpone until later periods the burden of payment for current outlay' (Buchanan and Congleton 1998, p. 10). Whatever else is said, intergenerational discrimination is clearly violative of the generality principle. Neither Ricardian equivalence nor the fact that public capital investment may yield intertemporal benefits and costs can justify this discrimination.[16] The irremediable fact is that future generations - those which cannot agree to bear the future costs of debt-financed government outlays - must be treated impartially. The institutional imperative is, therefore, a constitutional balanced budget constraint. Moreover, in the case of the United States, the constraint must apply both to on- and off-budget federal programs.[17]

If the generality principle applies to government borrowing, it applies, *mutatis mutandis*, to taxation and to government outlays.

With respect to taxation, the functioning of majoritarian democracy virtually ensures the emergence of discriminatory treatment: 'Adjusted for relative group size, members of the exploiting majority have more to gain from tax discrimination against the rich than against middle or low-income groups' (Buchanan and Congleton 1998, p. 91). Yet, if tax rate progressivity is a predictable outcome of postconstitutional conflictual politics, the proliferation of preferential tax code provisions[18] may be attributed to the rent-seeking activity of special interest groups.

It is clear that a progressive tax rate structure is inconsistent with the generality or impartiality standard and, *pari passu*, with the external morality of law (S 6.3). Equally important, preferential tax code provisions - many of which are surreptitiously legislated - are not reconcilable with the internal morality of law (S 6.3).

While I agree that political efficiency - the minimization of rent seeking - is an appropriate desideratum, the central issue is the discriminatory treatment of morally equivalent persons. Given that the 'ultimate purpose [of the generality norm] is to constrain majoritarian politics in order to prevent the natural tendency to use the taxing authority discriminatorialy' (Buchanan and Congleton 1998, p. 93), the institutional imperative is a constitutional generality or impartiality constraint. While Rawls has argued that 'since the burden of taxation is to be justly shared ... a proportional expenditure tax may be part of the best tax scheme' (1971, p. 278), a proportional tax defined on *all* income would also satisfy the impartiality standard.

Discussion of on- and off-budget outlays is complicated by the fact that governments engage in the production, distribution, and financing of pure public and potentially partitionable and excludable goods and services. Moreover, governments frequently engage in credit and insurance activities. In the United States, federal credit and insurance programs are intended both to '[help] disadvantaged groups' and to correct 'market failures' (Office of Management and Budget, *Analytical Perspectives*, 2003, p. 189). Of particular interest are direct loans and loan guarantees contemplating such disparate activities as housing, education, business and community development, and exports.[19] For their part, federal insurance programs underwrite bank, thrift and credit union deposits, guarantee private defined-benefit pension plans, and insure against such 'natural disasters' as floods and crop failure.[20] Whatever else is said, it is clear that 'targeted' credit and insurance programs - whether on- or off-budget - implicate the production and distribution of excludable goods.

Consider, first, the implications of government provision of public goods. As is well known, the Pigovian efficiency standard is typically deployed to argue for their provision. Central to the argument is the notion that a first-best Paretian outcome requires that public goods be financed by taxes which are levied on the 'marginal benefit principle'. On this logic, when tastes or technological conditions are not homogeneous, optimal government provision of pure public goods requires tax-price discrimination (Buchanan [1962] 1999, p. 71).[21]

While much can be said about this, it is essential first to recognize that, insofar as generality or impartiality requires that public good demanders pay *equal* cost shares, the Pigovian efficiency standard cannot be satisfied. Yet it is also clear that technical and political considerations militate against the application of the marginal benefit principle.[22] The essential idea is that there is no assurance that government provision of public goods and services can, in Pigovian logic, 'solve' the externality problem. Granting this, there is no *a priori* reason to suppose that government 'ought' to supply such goods. Yet, when public goods *are* produced by government, both the logic of rent seeking and the moral equivalence of persons imply a constitutional imperative: While the generality or impartiality standard does not determine the optimal tax base, the proceeds of a *uniform* tax rate imposed on that base should be earmarked for the provision of pure public goods or services (Buchanan and Congleton 1998, pp. 114-15).

In the United States more than 25 percent of federal government outlays implicates either intermediate demand for, or the production of, excludable goods.[23] Consider first the federal government's demand for inputs in such disparate production functions as 'national defense' and 'the administration of justice'. Reduced to its essentials, generality or impartiality requires that 'the production, itself, of government services should not materially alter the distribution of wealth. Thus, complete generality requires the absence of significant relative price effects in the production of government services' (Buchanan and Congleton 1998, p. 110).

If technical and market considerations[24] may militate against dispersion of government input demand, it is also clear that supplier rent seeking is endemic to the production process. Granting this, *political* efficiency, the moral equivalence of persons, and the internal morality of law (S 6.3) demand that *departures* from the generality standard be *publicly* justified. *Inter alia*, this underscores the efficacy of a constitutional prohibition against 'omnibus' laws (S 6.4).

If its demand for productive inputs must be constitutionally constrained, the same is true of government's indirect involvement in the production of excludable goods. In the United States, for example, agricultural programs are intended both to provide an 'economic safety net for farmers and ranchers, and ... [to] open, expand, and maintain global market opportunities for agricultural production' (Office of Management and Budget, *Budget*, 2001, p. 53).[25]

Under United States law the 'economic safety net' takes the form of income-support payments and direct and guaranteed loans.[26] Because they are inherently discriminatory, these programs both encourage rent seeking activity and are violative of the generality principle. It follows that both political efficiency and the moral equivalence of persons demand that such *discriminatory* transfer programs be constitutionally prohibited. Granting this, when, at the constitutional stage, agreement emerges that transfer or redistribution schemes should be institutionalized (Buchanan [1967] 1999, p. 298), impartiality requires that it take a particular form. While more will be said of this below, the essential idea is that 'A flat tax on all income combined with a set of equal-per-head demogrants would perhaps come closest to meeting the generality criterion. ...' (Buchanan and Congleton 1998, p. 118).

If the generality or impartiality principle has implications for agricultural policy's 'economic safety net' goal, the same is true of its foreign trade promotion imperative. *Inter alia*, trade promotion activities include 'subsidies to export firms', and 'credit guarantees for the commercial financing of U.S. agricultural exports' (Office of Management and Budget, *Budget*, 2001, pp. 55-6).

It is obvious that, *whatever* their motivation, 'trade promotion' activities are inherently discriminatory. It follows, *pari passu*, that generality requires either that such activities be constitutionally prohibited, or that *all* producers should, under the constitution, be accorded equal treatment. Both the moral equivalence of persons and the rent seeking associated with 'trade policy' suggest the efficacy of this institutional imperative.

Recall now that, in the United States, 'Federal credit programs offer direct loans and loan guarantees for a wide range of activities, primarily housing, education, business and rural development, and exports' (Office of Management and Budget, *Analytical Perspectives*, 2003, p. 189).

The fact that the United States government deploys 'market imperfection' or Paretian inefficiency arguments to 'justify' these programs is, itself, a matter of interest and concern.[27] On the one hand, there can be no presumption that, in the presence of market imperfections, government can do better (Roth 2002, pp. 43-52). On the other hand, the indeterminacy of the efficiency frontier suggests that Paretian - as opposed to political - efficiency is an inappropriate standard for public policy appraisal (S 4.7).

That said, the issue of immediate concern is neither the alleged Paretian efficiency of such programs nor the *political* inefficiency or rent seeking to which they inevitably give rise. Rather, the central issue is the in-period and intergenerational discrimination inherent in government credit programs. In the case of the former, it is tautological that credit programs favor 'targeted sectors' and, *pari passu,* 'targeted', individual beneficiaries. Yet there is a sense in which intergenerational discrimination is the decisive issue. Because agreement of future generations cannot be secured, members of current and future generations are not temporally equivalent. Given this brute fact, the moral equivalence of persons implies an institutional imperative: Whatever their avowed 'social purpose', government credit programs must be constitutionally prohibited.

If government credit programs must be generality constrained, the same is true of government risk underwriting activity. As before, the policy of the United States government is heuristic. With the 'role' of its insurance (and credit) programs characterized as 'helping disadvantaged groups and correcting market failures', the federal government 'insures bank, thrift, and credit union deposits, guarantees private defined-benefit pensions, and insures against other risks such as natural disasters, all up to certain limits' (Office of Management and Budget, *Analytical Perspectives*, 2003, p. 189). Familiarly, the presumption is that these programs can be justified by the presence of such 'market imperfections' as information opaqueness, externalities, resource constraints and imperfect competition (p. 190).

Without further justificatory argument, I suggest that the market imperfection argument is unavailing. The issue of interest is, instead, the moral imperative to manage government insurance programs impartially. While it is true that 'ex post differentiation is the nature of all true insurance programs' (Buchanan and Congleton 1998, p. 132), what is important, from the generality perspective, is that expected benefits be uniformly distributed among the electorate in an *ex ante* sense. Simply stated, the requirement is that 'each insured contingency is equally likely, and equally valued by all within the polity of interest' (p. 132).

Adherence to the generality principle is clearly difficult in this setting. Rent seeking and majoritarian cycling are likely to center, *inter alia*, on benefits, on tax prices, and on the probabilities of occurrence of random events. Moreover, expected benefits are likely, in the case of flood and crop insurance, to be concentrated in particular local polities. Finally, *ceteris paribus*, varying degrees of risk aversion imply that actuarially identical insurance programs 'may ... yield different expected net benefits for more or less risk-averse individuals' (Buchanan and Congleton 1998, p. 133).

What, then, may be said of the federal government's risk underwriting activities? While deposit insurance appears, in the *ex ante* sense, roughly to satisfy the generality principle, defined-benefit pension guarantees and flood and crop insurance are inherently discriminatory.

I observe, first, that because many individuals have access neither to defined-benefit nor to defined-contribution pension plans, the *ex ante* generality constraint cannot be satisfied.[28] It follows, therefore, that 'targeted' pension guarantees must be constitutionally prohibited. Second, it is clear on *a priori* grounds that the benefits of flood, crop and other 'disaster' insurance accrue to particular, localized members of the polity. Granting this, expected benefits cannot, in the *ex ante* sense, be uniformly distributed among the national polity. Yet, if the generality principle cannot be satisfied at the *federal* level, it is clear that 'A federalized structure of government can provide heterogeneous services while satisfying the strictures of generality' (Buchanan and Congleton 1998, p.

137). Granting this, both political efficiency and the moral equivalence of persons suggest that, when *ex ante* expected benefits cannot be uniformly distributed, the constitution prohibit *central* government goods or service provision. In the instant case, flood and crop insurance should have to be provided by state or local governments. *Inter alia*, this would prevent potential beneficiaries from shifting the burden of service provision to all members of the national polity. Equally important, given Tiebout-type mobility, competition among political jurisdictions would enhance the probability that 'local governments should be observed widely to provide substantially uniform service packages ... .' (p. 141).

Finally, my discussion of on- and off-budget tax and spending programs would be incomplete were I not to acknowledge what Buchanan and Congleton have characterized as the bias in favor of direct transfers over public goods financing (1998, p. 119).

While the increasing share of total United States government outlays attributable to means tested entitlements, Medicare and Social Security is consistent with this view,[29] this is not my immediate concern. Neither does my interest center on the rent seeking which is characteristic of transfer programs.[30] It is not, in short, the political inefficiency of transfer programs which is decisive. Rather, it is that transfer programs - except, in one sense, those directed toward 'the old' - are fundamentally discriminatory. Recognizing that all persons 'get old' and, therefore, that 'all persons are eventually eligible for program benefits' (Buchanan and Congleton 1998, p. 122), the generality standard is, in principle, satisfied. That said, means tested transfer programs are incommensurable with the standard.[31]

From the conservative's perspective, given the propensity to affect income transfers, the discriminatory bias inherent in postconstitutional, majoritarian politics and, above all, the moral equivalence of persons, the constitutional imperative is clear: If transfer or redistribution programs are financed through general tax revenues, a constitutional generality constraint must contemplate 'a flat tax on all income combined with a set of equal-per-head demogrants' (Buchanan and Congleton 1998, p. 118).[32]

If in-period transfer programs must be generality constrained, transfers from the currently employed to 'the old' must be subject to a constitutional, intertemporal generality constraint. While it is true that all persons eventually become eligible for publicly financed retirement programs, it is also true that political and technical considerations militate against the impartial treatment of morally equivalent retired persons. We know, for example, that retired persons are subject to the vagaries of contingent circumstance; in particular, to the preferences of successive median voters who, under pay-as-you-go public pension plans, must absorb the cost of intergenerational transfers. Moreover, changing birth rates and longer life spans may exert upward pressure on tax rates, and downward pressure on retirement benefits. Under the circumstances envisioned, it is not implausible to assume that majoritarian distributional conflict will emerge.[33] Granting this, 'Intertemporal programs have to ensure equal treatment through time if they are to satisfy the generality principle. This implies that, once enacted, essentially they become permanent' (Buchanan and Congleton 1998, p. 124). Given that demographic and technological changes militate against an invariant tax-benefit structure it follows that

> Effective constitutionalization would suggest that tax rates (or age for eligibility) move upward if the ratio tilts unexpectedly toward a higher number of prospective retirees because of increased life expectancy and that transfer payments move downward if the ratio tilts because of declines in birth rates. Such a rule would violate intergenerational generality but would preserve the fiscal viability of the public pension system. (pp. 126-7)

In the conservative view, a constitutional rule, rather than postconstitutional, majoritarian politics should animate programmatic changes.

6.6   OFF-OFF-BUDGET ACTIVITY

In the peculiar vernacular of Washington, 'off-off-budget' activity contemplates federal regulatory policy initiatives (US Congress Joint Economic Committee 1979, pp. 53-4). As measured by one admittedly crude index, federal off-off-budget activity is expanding. Between calendar 2000 and 2002 the number of pages in the *Federal Register* increased from 74,528 to 75,606 (Lee 2003, p. A15). Moreover, recent data suggest that federal agencies promulgate more regulations than does the United States Congress. In calendar 2002 '4,167 proposed and final regulations were issued [by agencies], while the president signed into law 269 bills passed by Congress' (Cusack 2003, p. 11).[34]

While the volume and sources of regulatory policy impulses have been catalysts to a large and growing literature, my interest centers on the rent seeking which characterizes the regulatory 'process'.

I stipulate, first, that the first fundamental welfare theorem is often deployed to rationalize government market interventions (S 4.5). The inclination to invoke the theorem persists despite the fact that there can be no presumption that, in the face of 'market failure', the government can do better (Roth 2002, pp. 43-52). *Inter alia*, even if one grants the existence of the efficiency frontier, the general theorem of the second best 'show[s] the futility of "piecemeal welfare economics"' (Lipsey and Lancaster 1956, p. 17).[35] Yet, as we have seen (S 4.7), the efficiency frontier and, *mutatis mutandis*, the efficiency standard, are indeterminate. Granting this, regulatory interventions animated by the familiar Paretian efficiency or welfare conditions may properly be characterized as *ad hoc*.

With all of this as background, there is a sense in which the logical, empirical and ontological problems associated with the first and second fundamental welfare theorems are irrelevant.[36] At issue are government interventions in domestic and international markets motivated by rent seeking rather than by the fundamental welfare theorems. Because they are both politically inefficient and inherently discriminatory such interventons are, from the conservative's perspective, indefensible.

Rent seeking 'demand for regulation' in America's domestic markets has become commonplace. The Trans-Alaska Pipeline Act of 1973 required that Alaskan crude oil be transported in US-flag vessels (Kumins 1995). The Disadvantaged Business Enterprise program managed by the Transportation Department mandates construction project 'set-asides' for certain 'qualified' individuals (Fields 2001, p. A14). The United States Department of Agriculture's Navel Orange Administrative Committee imposes restrictions on orange sales - presumably 'at the behest of Sunkist, which dominates the California-Arizona citrus market' (Bovard 1995, p. 53), and the National Labor Relations Board 'will punish corporations - and impose injunctions - if the NLRB suspects that a pay raise for workers is not in a union's best interests'(Bovard 1999, p. 158).[37]

If these 'economic' and 'social regulations'[38] are animated by the concentrated benefit-dispersed cost calculus, they also reflect what has been characterized as an institutional overclaiming problem. In effect, a 'lobby can go to the ... legislature and say, "Let us have our way. You're not going to have to pay for this"' (Epstein 1992, p. 9).[39]

While the *political* efficiency argument for a constitutional constraint on economic rent-animated regulation is compelling, more is ultimately at issue. Insofar as these 'interferences with domestic trade cannot be justified ... on the basis of either externality or public good arguments' (Buchanan and Congleton 1998, p. 77), it is their intendedly discriminatory nature which is decisive. Given that they are incommensurable with the moral equivalence of persons they must be constitutionally prohibited.

If domestic producers seek 'protection' from foreign competition,[40] exporters are also rent seekers. The United States' experience is heuristic:

> Seven federal agencies, the Department of Agriculture ..., the Department of Defense, the Department of State, the Department of the Treasury, the Agency for International Development ..., the Export-Import Bank, and the Overseas Private Investment Corporation ..., provide direct loans, loan guarantees, and insurance to a variety of foreign private and sovereign borrowers. These programs are intended to level the playing field for U.S. exporters, deliver robust support for U.S. manufactured goods, stabilize international financial markets, and promote sustainable development. (Office of Management and Budget, *Analytical Perspectives*, 2001, pp. 154-5)[41]

While it is possible to argue that 'the government' establishes trade policy, in part, by taking account of 'social welfare' (Mitra 1999), I associate myself with the 'protection for sale' model suggested by Grossman and Helpman (1994). On the one hand, the indeterminancy of social welfare theory (SS 4.7 and 4.9) calls into question the normative use of the first and second fundamental welfare theorems. On the other hand, the economic rents associated with import restraints and government-subsidized export promotion are indisputable.

Granting this, both the political inefficiency inherent in external market interventions and the moral equivalence of persons suggest an institutional imperative: The body of 'trade law' must be nondiscriminatory. The question of immediate interest is, How might this be achieved? While a uniform tariff rate imposed on all imports appears to satisfy the impartiality principle, in fact it would be discriminatory. Reduced to its essentials, 'it discriminates overtly against those producing interests that seek only to enter exchanges in domestic markets or to sell to foreigners. And any such restriction also discriminates against ... consumers' (Buchanan and Congleton 1998, p. 80). For their part, if it is clear that export subsidies discriminate against producers that sell only in domestic markets, direct and guaranteed loans to foreign borrowers - whether private or sovereign - impose indirect and, in the case of defaults, direct costs on taxpayers. On this logic, the institutional imperative is clear: Given the indeterminacy of consequentialist social welfare theory, external market interventions cannot be 'scientifically' justified. Rather, they must be understood to be a reflection of the concentrated benefit-dispersed cost calculus. It follows, therefore, that *all* external market interventions must be constitutionally prohibited.

The indeterminancy of the first and second fundamental welfare theorems notwithstanding, it seems clear that *apparent* divergences between private and social cost will continue to animate 'environmental' and other policies. This is true, moreover, despite the conceptual and empirical problems associated with these concepts (Roth 2002, pp. 45-7).

Given that generalized externalities - whether 'measurable' or not - are an objective feature of observable reality it is important to acknowledge the *political* efficiency of a generality constraint on environmental law. Simply stated, asymmetric treatment of different sources of identical effluents 'open[s] environmental law up to the machinations of majoritarian politics and special interest groups while increasing enforcement and adherence costs' (Buchanan and Congleton 1998, p. 65).[42]

Some may, of course, object that, in this setting, Paretian efficiency losses may offset the political efficiency gains associated with an operative generality constraint. If the presence of nonreciprocal externalities enhances the probability of such a tradeoff (Buchanan and Congleton 1998, pp. 65-9), this *possibility* cannot be decisive. First, as been repeatedly emphasized, the indeterminancy of the efficiency standard militates against its normative use. Second, the case for a generality constraint is enhanced when account is taken of the complexities inherent in path-dependent phenomena:

> in cases in which technological or other changes affect the payoffs of externality generating activities or create new unanticipated possibilities, the ideal pattern, range and domain of use rights change through time, often in ways that cannot be anticipated. So long as political decisions have to be reached on such matters, there remains an important role for the generality principle as a guide to policy formation. (Buchanan and Congleton 1998, p. 75)

Finally, if political efficiency is justificatory of appeal to a constitutional generality constraint, the external and internal morality of law demands it (S 6.3).

Granting all of this, the constitution must require that identical sources of generalized externalities be treated symmetrically.

6.7   THE IMPLICATIONS FOR ECONOMICS

Following Dworkin's definitional scheme (1985, p. 184), the derivative positions adumbrated above are valued as strategies for the achievement of the conservative's constitutive political positions. The latter, valued for their own sake, are the subject matter of Chapter 5. While the constitutive positions need not be reprised here, I emphasize, again, their Kantian roots.

Central to the conservative's enterprise is Kant's first- and third-person points of view (SS 3.2 and 5.3). For the conservative, as for Kant, the motive to respect the imperative to treat morally equivalent persons equally cannot be generated by the autonomous, transcendental, first-person self. Roughly congruent with Adam Smith's 'civilizing project' (S 1.3), the essential idea is that it is societal influence - the immediate 'ought' of family and other social attachments - which animates both the motive to treat others as ends rather than as means and the other dimensions of moral argument and appraisal. *Inter alia*, 'examples of honesty of purpose, of steadfastness in following good maxims, of sympathy and general benevolence' (Kant [1785] 1988, p. 87) can cultivate what Roger Scruton has called ordinary conscience (S 5.4). In effect, the 'better person', the third-person self which the agent 'imagines himself to be' (p. 87) is able 'to overcome the promptings of all heteronomous counsels, such as those of self-interest and desire' (Scruton 1982, p. 65) only if 'He is a creature of extended sympathies, motivated by love, admiration, shame, and a host of other social emotions' (Scruton 1996, p. 114).[43]

If the idea of the social cultivation of moral sentiments is central to the conservative's constitutive and derivative political positions, it finds no expression in the body of mainstream, neoclassical economic theory. Institutionless and intendedly value-free, the theory is grounded in a peculiar conception of self, *homo economicus* (S 4.6). Autonomous, atomistic, narrowly self-interested, relentlessly utilitarian and fully informed, economic man's preference structure is consistently ordered, exogenously determined, and intertemporally stable. Equally important, formal and informal institutions, including behavioral norms, play no role in shaping economic man's decision environment.

While, from the perspective of the logical positivist, all of this is unexceptionable, the parable ignores 'a recurrent theme in economics ... that the values to which people respond are not confined to those one would expect based on the narrowly defined canons of rationality' (Smith 2003, p. 465).[44] Moreover, neither economic man nor the liberal's transcendental, autonomous self construal can be reconciled with objective features of observable reality:

> most of our operating knowledge, and ability to decide and perform is nondeliberative. Our brains conserve attentional, conceptual, and symbolic thought resources because they are scarce, and proceeds to delegate most decision-making to automatic processes

(including the emotions) that do not require conscious attention .... This leads to an alternative, ecological concept of rationality: an emergent order based on trial-and-error cultural and biological evolutionary processes. It yields home- and socially grown rules of action, traditions and moral principles that underlie property rights in impersonal exchange, and social cohesion in personal exchange. (Smith 2003, pp. 499-500)

However it is styled, this understanding of cognitive and decision processes emphasizes the need to return to economic's roots; to a conception of agents immersed in contingent circumstance, both affecting and affected by, society's evolving formal and informal institutions.

This, as we have seen, is a conservative conception. It is, moreover, congruent with the work of the constitutional political economist (S 5.5). These ideas inform the discussion in Chapter 7.

NOTES

1.   See Sections 3.2, 3.4, 4.2 and 5.4
2.   For more on the distinction between utilitarianism - a telelogical theory - and Kant's deontological theory, see Rawls (1971, p. 30).
3.   See, for example, Buchanan (1987, pp. 249-50).
4.   For more on the original position and the veil of ignorance, see Rawls (1971, pp. 12, 190 and 456), Kymlicka (1993, p. 193) and Hampton (1995, p. 387).
5.   The justification for such limits must be that they 'protect other freedoms' (Rawls 1971, p. 229). Thus, for example, 'A bill of rights may remove certain liberties from majority regulation altogether, and the separation of powers with judicial review may slow down the pace of legislative change' (p. 228). It is noteworthy that Rawls' judicial review conception comports with the conservative view that, 'in the fever of fomented change, the [independent] judiciary must act as a conservative force' (Scruton 2002, p. 58). In effect, an independent judiciary must serve to protect citizens 'from the state's encroachments' (p. 175).
6.   As we have seen (S 1.3), attempts by groups and individuals to promote their own interests was one of Adam Smith's central concerns. See, for example, Smith ([1776] 1976, pp. 452-72).
7.   *Inter alia*, 'A conscientious effort must be made to determine whether an infraction has taken place and to impose the correct penalty' (Rawls 1971, pp. 238-9). See Section 3.4 for a discussion of natural and social justice.
8.   I have in mind, for example, the House and Senate Rules Committees which determine the procedures under which bills will be considered.
9.   See, for example, Furubotn and Richter (1997, pp. 128-9).
10. See, for example, Bovard (1999, pp. 110-11).
11. It must be acknowledged, of course, that 'even the ideal legislature is an imperfect procedure. There seems to be no way to characterize a feasible procedure guaranteed to lead to just legislation' (Rawls 1971, p. 360; see also p. 362).
12. See also Rawls (1971, Chapter 6, especially p. 334).
13. A body of survey, poll and other evidence has led James Bovard to suggest that 'If citizen comprehension of government and public affairs is the currency of democracy, America is long since bankrupt' (1999, p. 105).
14. Office of Management and Budget, *A Citizen's Guide to the Federal Budget*, 2001, p. 34. See also Office of Management and Budget, *Analytical Perspectives*, 2003, pp. 474-5.
15. Federal law requires that Social Security and other 'trust fund' balances be invested in Treasury debt securities (Office of Management and Budget, *Analytical Perspectives*, 2003, p. 370).

16. In principle, future tax sources could be earmarked to service and amortize investment project-related costs (Buchanan and Congleton, 1998, p. 101; see also pp. 99-100).

17. The generality principle applies with equal force to debt retirement:

> Why should any particular generation of taxpayers be singled out for differentially high taxation, without corresponding benefits, in order to reduce the tax obligations of ... future generations? The generality principle emerges here as a relatively powerful argument against any policy of debt retirement. The 'sins of the past' ... should be borne equally across all generations (Buchanan and Congleton 1998, p. 102).

18. I have in mind the special exclusions, exemptions, deductions, special tax credits, tax deferrals, and preferential tax rates applied to disparate 'tax bases' which have come to characterize the United States Tax Code. For an adumbration of the nature and estimated cost of such 'tax expenditures' see Office of Management and Budget, *Analytical Perspectives*, 2003, pp. 101-40.

19. For a discussion of credit programs in these 'sectors', see Office of Management and Budget, *Analytical Perspectives*, 2003, pp. 196-208.

20. Recently, the federal government has provided 'insurance against terrorism and other security-related risks'. See Office of Management and Budget, *Analytical Perspectives*, 2003, pp. 189 and 212-13.

21. See also Buchanan ([1968] 1999, p. 32).

22. See, for example, Roth (2002, pp. 47-8).

23. For a detailed discussion, see Roth (2002, pp. 89-91). See also Office of Management and Budget, *Historical Tables*, 2003, especially p. 115.

24. Transaction-specific investments, factor immobility, locational economies and size of market are examples.

25. Interestingly, while it acknowledges that 'government payments are not necessarily reaching the producers that most need them', and that 'Commodity payments are important to agricultural producers, but sometimes they distort the market', the Bush Administration 'Continues implementation of [the] farm program safety net, with [a] 10-year cost of $174 billion' (Office of Management and Budget, *Budget*, 2003, pp. 57, 58 and 55).

26. During fiscal year 2002 federal government 'mandatory [agricultural] outlays' exceeded 49.2 billion dollars, while direct loan disbursements and guaranteed loans totaled, respectively, 15.9 and 9.9 billion dollars (Office of Management and Budget, *Budget*, 2003, p. 65).

27. See, for example, Office of Management and Budget, *Analytical Perspectives*, 2003, pp. 189-0).

28. The United States government acknowledges that 'The number of active workers in [Pension Benefit Guaranty Corporation]-covered plans fell from 27 million in calendar 1985 to fewer than 23 million in calendar 2000 ... . If the trend continues, active workers may constitute less than half of PBGC - insured participants in calendar 2003' (Office of Management and Budget, *Analytical Perspectives*, 2003, p. 209.

29. See Office of Management and Budget, *Historical Tables*, 2003, p. 125.

30. See, for example, Buchanan and Congleton (1998, p. 122).

31. The point is not that means testing promotes rent seeking (Buchanan and Congleton 1998, pp. 120-21). It is that means testing is itself discriminatory.

32. Equal-per-head demogrants must also apply to the direct or subsidized provision of in-kind services such as medical care. While pressure to depart from generality may emanate both from prospective beneficiaries and from service providers, 'genuine constitutionalization of all such in-kind programs can be helpful in attenuating the potential distributional conflict' (Buchanan and Congleton 1998, p. 125).

33. *Inter alia*, 'means testing becomes politically attractive because it reduces the financial claims on the system' (Buchanan and Congleton 1998, p. 127).

34. See also Bovard (1995, p. 1)

35. The point is that, while 'regulatory' policy may be *informed* by general equilibrium theory, explicit account cannot be taken of all of the interrelationships which define an economy (Salanié 2000, p. 138). It follows, *pari passu*, that all regulatory interventions are 'piecemeal'.

36. For a discussion of the second fundamental welfare theorem, see S 4.9.

37. A defense bill passed by the US House of Representatives in May 2003 requires that 'at least 65 percent of the components in items purchased by the Pentagon be American-made, up from the current level of 50 percent'. As might be expected, 'Labor unions, including ship-builders, and specific industries that stand to benefit from the House language, like American titanium manufacturers, are supporting the measure' (Snyder 2003). Should the bill become law it will institutionalize both internal and external market interventions.

38. For a discussion of the distinction between the two, see Council of Economic Advisers (1989, p. 190).

39. It is also clear that 'social' regulation is an 'increasingly attractive mechanism for redistributing wealth, given fiscal constraints' (Hahn 1998, especially p. 209).

40. A recent - and prominent - example is the Bush Administration's decision in March 2002 to impose a 30 percent tariff on imported steel. For an appreciation of steel users' reaction, see King (2002). For other examples of import restraints, including anti-dumping penalties, see Bovard (1995, pp. 57-61) and Bovard (1999, pp. 155-7).

41. For a list of the top ten corporate beneficiaries of Export-Import Bank loans, guarantees and insurance see Phillips and Heinauer (2001). While the World Trade Organization has ruled them illegal, US exporters also benefit from a tax break intended to lower their prices on world markets. For a list of the top ten beneficiaries of the Foreign Sales Corporation tax benefit see Murray and King (2003).

42. The same logic applies, *mutatis mutandis*, to positive externalities. Logical, empirical and other problems aside, identical sources of such externalities must be treated symmetrically.

43. See also Smith ([1759] 1976, pp. 320-21 and S 1.3).

44. For more on this, see S 4.6.

7. Toward a Conservative Economics

7.1 *HOMO ECONOMICUS* AND THE FIRST-PERSON SELF

While, to my knowledge, no explicit account has been taken of it, there are elements of rough correspondence between orthodox, neoclassical economics' *homo economicus* conception, and the liberal's transcendental, autonomous self construal. Both regard the agent as autonomous and atomistic. Equally important, meddlesome, nosy or external preferences present a problem for both construals.

While *homo economicus* is regarded as a narrowly self-interested, fully-informed utility maximizer, it is recognized that, if they are present, interpersonal effects in utility functions are problematic. In particular, if minimal privacy rights are respected, meddlesome or nosy preferences militate against the specification of a social welfare function. This, in turn, calls into question the normative use of the second fundamental welfare theorem (S 4.9).

If meddlesome or nosy preferences are incommensurable with the economist's theory of the state, they are inimical to the self-realization of the liberal's transcendental, autonomous self. Indeed, it is this concern which animates the 'natural rights' as trumps against 'external - or political, altruistic, or moralistic - preferences' construction (SS 1.2, 1.4 and 3.3).

Semantics aside, the meddlesome, nosy or metapreferences which trouble the economic theorist subsume the same phenomena contemplated by the liberal's external preferences construal. It follows that external preferences are a shared problem. Interestingly, however, the problem arises for the economist when minimal privacy rights *are* respected. For the liberal, the 'solution' contemplates respect for 'natural rights' *against* such preferences.

The external preferences problem is a metaphor for a larger 'values' problem. While it is both institutionless and *intendedly* value-free, the economist's theory of the state is, in fact, a hybrid moral theory. Because it is utilitarian, it is consequentialist or outcomes-based. Yet, because unattenuated property and exchange rights are instrumentally important to the achievement of first-best Paretian outcomes, it incorporates elements of a right-based moral theory. Difficulties arise because the theory cannot accommodate the moral force of rights (SS 3.3 and 4.3). Moreover, the theory cannot accommodate any plausible theory of justice (S 4.10). Granting all of this, the economist's theory of the state is an untenable moral theory (SS 4.3 and 4.10).

For its part, the liberal's self-legislating, transcendental self, ensconced behind a 'natural rights' structure, is free to erect his own, subjective, moral code. If it is true that the moral pluralism and institutional skepticism to which this conception gives rise is a 'devious form of the moral law', it is also true that the liberal's transcendental, autonomous, first-person self has no motive to act (SS 5.3 and 5.4). For this, he must - as Kant insisted - invoke his 'empirical self': a self both animated and constrained by contingent circumstance. Among the defining characteristics of such an environment are the formal and informal institutions which characterize a society. And central among these are the sources of moral argument and appraisal which, unlike the Moral Law, are not endogenous to the individual. Reflective of a 'web of attachments', the ethic of virtue, sympathy and piety are themselves instrumentally, perhaps intrinsically, valuable to social cohesion. Yet neither *homo economicus* nor the transcendental, first-person self is informed, animated, or constrained by these elements of 'ordinary conscience' (S 5.4). It remains now to develop the implications for economic theory.

7.2 SOME METHODOLOGICAL PRELIMINARIES

I suggest, without further justificatory argument that, for the conservative, the 'values problem' is determinative. *Inter alia*, the economist's theory of the state, and the *homo economicus* construal on which it is based, must be rejected. Consequence-based and procedurally-detached, the theory is both indeterminate (SS 4.7 and 4.9) and incommensurable with the Kantian perspective which informs conservative thinking (SS 4.2 and 5.5).

The balance of this chapter is motivated by three, related, ideas: First, 'no economic theory makes proper sense until conjoined to some adequate political doctrine (a doctrine which defines the nature and rights of the social arrangement to be served)' (Scruton 2002, pp. 106-7). Second, economic theory must take explicit account of the path-dependency of persons' preference and value structures, and of the endogeneity of formal and informal institutions. Third, given its Kantian roots, 'conservative' economics must be procedurally-based and consequence-detached. It must, in conception and execution, be the opposite of orthodox, neoclassical economic theory.

With discussion of the first and third ideas momentarily deferred, interest centers on the second.

Recall, first, that the empirical content of the *homo economicus* construal has been the subject of persistent and vigorous attack (S 4.6).[1] It is a matter of the first importance that the patent unrealism of the construction has mattered little to its defenders. Without question, this posture is animated by neoclassical economists' commitment to 'The Methodology of Positive Economics' (Friedman 1953, pp. 3-43).[2] The claim is that 'Economics is a positive science' (p. 39) in the sense suggested by John Neville Keynes. It is, in short, 'a body of systematized knowledge concerning what is', rather than a normative science, or 'a body of systematized knowledge discussing criteria of what ought to be'.[3] Given that it is a 'positive science', 'economics is in principle independent of any particular ethical position or normative judgements ... . In short, positive economics is, or can be, an "objective" science, in precisely the same sense as any of the physical sciences' (p. 4).

If the assertion that economics is a positive science accounts for the propensity of neoclassical economists implicitly or explicitly to ignore the intervention of ethical - and other - societal norms, it is the 'as if' construal which accounts for their willingness to ignore, or to discount, the patent 'unrealism' of assumptions:

> It is an accepted hypothesis that ... the distance traveled by a falling body in any specified time is given by the formula $s = 1/2gt^2$, where s is the distance traveled in feet and t is time in seconds. The application of this formula to a compact ball dropped from the roof of a building is equivalent to saying that a ball so dropped behaves *as if* it were falling in a vacuum. (Friedman 1953, p. 16)

Given that the purpose of a theory is *prediction*, Friedman insists that 'This example illustrates both the impossibility of testing a theory by its assumptions and also the ambiguity of the concept "the assumptions of a theory" ... . The formula is accepted because it works, not because we live in an approximate vacuum - whatever that means' (pp. 17-18).

Stripped to its essentials, the positivist - or instrumentalist - view holds that a theory is an instrument for prediction. Granting this, 'the only relevant test of the *validity* of a hypothesis is comparison of its predictions with experience' (pp. 8-9), not the descriptive realism of its assumptions (p. 15).[4]

I stipulate, first, that it is possible to argue - given Friedman's view of assumptions as *instruments* of *prediction* - that 'the distinction between realistic and unrealistic assumptions is at best irrelevant' (Nagel 1963, p. 218).[5] Yet, as Nagel has observed,

> an economic theory (e.g., the neoclassical theory of consumer choice) is a set of statements, organized in a characteristic way, and designed to serve as partial premises for explaining, as well as predicting an indeterminately large (and usually varied) class of economic phenomena. (1963, p. 212)[6]

Thus, if one sets out, as economists are wont to do, not only to predict but to explain[7] phenomena

> in terms of the mechanisms involved in their occurrence ... [the theory employed] cannot be viewed as [Friedman] suggests that it can, as a 'simple summary' of some vaguely delimited set of empirical generalizations with distinctly specified ranges of application. (Nagel 1963, p. 218)

What is required, in short, is a set of statements that specify correspondences between the expressions embodied in the theory and the empirically determinable features of actual processes (pp. 212-13).

Consider, for example, the presence in the neoclassical theory of demand of an unidentified *exogenous* variable. Here, economic man's 'private and unobservable' preference structure (Smith 2003, p. 477) is assumed to be both exogenously determined and intertemporally stable. Yet, unless the preference structure is known *a priori*,

> the set of events over which the law [of demand] is supposed to hold cannot be completely defined or identified. Accordingly, there is an insufficient number of interpretive rules to allow one to determine whether the behavior of the consumer is consistent with the law or not. (Clarkson 1963, p. 99)[8]

All of this has basic relevance to Friedman's 'as if' construal. As Nagel emphasizes (1963, p. 216), Friedman suggests (1953, p. 18) that the law of falling bodies can be restated to read: 'under a wide range of circumstances, bodies that fall in the actual atmosphere behave *as if* they were falling in a vacuum'. However, 'the proposed paraphrase mistakenly assumes Galileo's law can be assigned the functions actually performed by statements of correspondence' (Nagel 1963, p. 217). In point of fact, 'This "ideal" law is supposed to be true only for bodies falling *in vacuo* when near the earth's surface'. It follows that, 'In this case the interpretive rules [must] consist of a set of instructions that identify the factors to take into consideration, e.g., the density of the media, the shape of the object, etc., as well as the effect on the results' (Clarkson 1963, p. 74).

The essential point is that, given the absence of appropriate interpretive rules, the 'as if' construal is inherently ambiguous:

> consider the assertion that businessmen behave *as if* they were attempting to maximize profits, ... that under certain conditions businessmen behave *as if* they were attempting to maximize profits. Given the requisite circumstances, if any, what can we predict, or in other words, what observable implications can we derive from this 'as if' statement? Unfortunately, no observable implications seem to follow. If businessmen act only *as if* trying to maximize profits, then evidently they do not exactly try to maximize profits, at least not all the time, and perhaps sometimes they do not try to maximize profits at all. As a result, no specific conclusions about businessmen's actions, however vague and tentative, can be strictly derived from this statement. (Melitz 1965, p. 50)[9]

The theoretical and empirical lacunae to which the 'as if' construal gives rise are the product of a methodological error. The suggestion that 'in general, the more significant the theory, the more unrealistic the assumptions' (Friedman 1953, p. 14) is fundamentally misleading. On the one hand, the realism of 'auxiliary' assumptions - statements which specify that which is assumed to be constant - is a *sine qua non* for the confirmation (disconfirmation) of a theory (Melitz 1965, p. 43). Roughly paraphrased, if that which is assumed to be constant is not, in fact, constant, accurate (inaccurate) predictions cannot be construed to be confirmatory (disconfirmatory) of a hypothesis. On the other hand, the realism of 'generative' assumptions - the set of statements which serve to derive a hypothesis, given the auxiliary assumptions - enhances the probability that derived hypotheses are true (pp. 46 and 52).[10] Stated differently,

> the more unrealistic these [generative] assumptions, the weaker the basis for relying on them in order to develop hypotheses or hunches. Hence, ... tests of economic assumptions are generally useful in testing and appraising hypotheses, and in indicating possible avenues of improvement in theory and hypotheses. (p. 52)[11]

If these considerations suggest that the 'as if' construal is untenable,[12] they also provide a standard against which the *homo economicus* construal may be appraised. Reduced to its essentials, the question is, Do the assumptions embodied in the paradigm provide the necessary statements of correspondence or, what is the same thing, are the generative and auxiliary assumptions realistic?

7.3   *HOMO ECONOMICUS*, AGAIN

I begin by stipulating that the argument developed in Section 4.6 need not be reprised. It is sufficient to emphasize that a growing body of evidence suggests that, in their market and non-market activity, humans are neither autonomous nor narrowly self-interested. Neither are they classically rational, fully-informed utility maximizers.[13] In fact, humans are 'social creatures' (Smith 2003, p. 466) for whom

> social context can be important in the interactive decision behavior we observe. This possibility follows from the autobiographical character of memory and the manner in which past encoded experience interacts with current sensory input in creating memory. (p. 487)

If this suggests that behavior is path-dependent, it also underscores the importance of past experience and cooperation in shaping behavior.

Recall, first, that the boundedly rational agent is subject to a competence-difficulty (C-D) gap (S 4.6). Given a 'gap between his competence and the difficulty of the decision problem to be solved' (Heiner 1983, p. 562), 'behavior patterns are *not* an approximation to maximizing so as to always choose most preferred alternatives (i.e., behaving "as if" an agent could successfully maximize with no C-D gap)' (p. 568).[14] Rather, what emerges is a pattern of '"rule-governed" behavior, such as instinct, habits, routines, rules of thumb, administrative procedures, customs, norms, and so forth' (p. 567).[15] The essential idea is that

> human activity is diffused and dominated by unconscious, autonomic, neuropsychological systems that enable people to function effectively without always calling upon the brain's scarcest resource - attentional and reasoning circuitry ... . Imagine the strain on the brain's resources if at the supermarket a shopper were required to explicitly evaluate his preferences for every combination of the tens of thousands of grocery items that are feasible for a given budget. Such mental processes are enormously opportunity - costly and implicitly our brain knows, if our conscious mind does not know, that we must avoid incurring opportunity costs that are not worth the benefit. The challenge of any unfamiliar action or problem appears first to trigger a search by the brain to bring to the conscious mind what one knows that is related to the decision context. Context triggers autobiographical experiential memory . (Smith 2003, pp. 468-9)[16]

If it is clear that none of this is reconcilable with the *homo economicus* and 'as if' construals, there is, for present purposes, an equally important dimension to the analysis: Rule-governed behavior is not restricted to the agent's market behavior. In a manner reminiscent of Adam Smith's 'civilizing project' (S 1.3),[17] 'people may use social-grown norms of trust and reciprocity ... to achieve cooperative states' (Smith 2003, p. 467).[18] Indeed, Vernon Smith insists that 'The pattern of [experimental economics] results greatly modifies the prevailing, and I believe misguided, rational [standard socioeconomic science model], and richly modernizes the unadulterated message of the Scottish philosophers' (p. 466).[19] Particular emphasis is placed on the implications for economics of the work of Hume and Adam Smith:

> An eighteenth-century precursor of Herbert Simon, David Hume was concerned with the limits of reason, the bounds on human understanding, and with scaling back the exaggerated claims of Cartesian constructivism. To Hume, rationality was phenomena that reason discovers in emergent institutions. Thus, 'the rules of morality ... are not conclusions of (our) reason' .... Adam Smith developed the idea of emergent order for economics. Truth is discovered in the form of the intelligence embodied in rules and traditions that have formed, inscrutably, out of the ancient history of human social interactions. This is the antithesis of the anthropocentric belief that if an observed social mechanism is functional, somebody in the unrecorded past must have used reason consciously to create it to serve its perceived intended purposes. (Smith 2003, p. 470)[20]

Whatever else is said, this is, in its essentials, a *conservative* construction. If *homo economicus* is effectively displaced, the liberal's transcendental, antonomous self is clearly absent. Instead, immersed in contingent, path-dependent circumstance, the agent both affects, and is affected by, the formal and informal institutions which define his society.[21]

Consider, for example, Vernon Smith's 'Proposition: ... collectives discover law in those rules that persist long enough to become entrenched practices' (2003, p. 484). While he proffers a number of illustrations of the proposition, the following is heuristic:

> The early 'law-givers' did not make the law they 'gave'; they studied social traditions and informal rules and gave voice to them, as God's, or natural, law. The common lawyer, Sir Edward Coke, championed seventeenth-century social norms as law commanding higher authority than the king. Remarkably, these forces prevailed, paving the way for the rule of law in England. (p. 484)

Interestingly, this characterization of the role of 'social traditions and informal rules' in shaping law is congruent with the conservative view that 'common law ... contains information that could not be contained in a legislative program. ... The example of common law gives the lie to the liberal scoffing at tradition' (Scruton 2002, pp. 32-3). The essential idea is that 'tradition ... is not a custom or a ritual but a form of social knowledge' (p. 31); a body of knowledge which, in turn, informs the common law and constitutional discourse.[22] The nexus between tradition and the evolution of formal institutions informs the conservative's view that neither 'the law' nor a constitution can be 'made' (p. 38). Because social knowledge - tradition - 'arises from the search over time for agreement' (p. 32), neither the law nor a constitution may be viewed as 'constructed' means to ends. Thus, whereas liberals 'point to the American constitution as proof of [the] contention [that a constitution can be made] ... the example is a bad one' (p. 38):

> It ignores the American inheritance, and the peculiar circumstances that led to drawing up a document designed both to secure the unity and to safeguard the eccentricities of the original participant states. It ignores all that language and custom had already established - in particular the tradition of English common law which both preceded and survived the break with the Crown ... . It ignores the already constituted rights and liberties which made the conscious adoption of a 'constitution' into a coherent gesture. It ignores the logic of common-law jurisdiction, which entails that the American Constitution is not contained in a single document but in four hundred volumes of intricate case law. In short, it ignores the fact that the written constitution of the United States - like any written constitution - is an abstract formula. (pp. 38-9)

The elements of rough correspondence between Scruton's 'American inheritance' and Vernon Smith's 'social traditions and informal rules' formulations is striking. Yet, whatever else is said, the essential, shared idea is that cooperation - and social cohesion - is animated by the path-dependent intervention of emergent customs, traditions, and social and moral behavioral norms.[23] If this is apparent to conservatives, and if it has, '[h]istorically, [been] a recurrent theme in economics' (Smith 2003, p. 465), it is an idea that is foreign to orthodox, neoclassical economic theory. What is required is a 'second concept of rational order, as an undesigned ecological system that emerges out of cultural and biological evolutionary processes: homegrown principles of action, norms, traditions, and "morality"' (pp. 469-70).[24] Thus, whereas the neoclassical economist deploys *homo economicus* and the 'as if' construal to predict - and, more heroically, to explain - behavior, the imperative is

> to examine the behavior of individuals based on their experience and folk knowledge, who are 'naive' in their ability to apply constructivist tools to the decisions they make; to understand the emergent order in human cultures; to discover the possible intelligence embodied in the rules, norms, and institutions of our cultural and biological heritage that are created from human interactions but not by deliberate human design. People follow rules without being able to articulate them, but they can be discovered. This is the intellectual heritage of the Scottish philosophers, who described and interpreted the social and economic order they observed. (Smith 2003, p. 470)[25]

The upshot is that the 'theoretical tractability' of the neoclassical paradigm[26] cannot compensate for its inability to account for the endogeneity of preference and value structures, the propensity to cooperate, and the role and importance of formal and informal institutions.[27] The root cause of these theoretical and empirical lacunae is neoclassical economists' intellectual commitment to 'positive' economics, to the 'as if' construal, and to the institutionless, *intendedly* value-free decision environment inhabited by *homo economicus*. On the one hand, the 'as if' construal is theoretically and empirically debilitating. *Inter alia*, it endorses and encourages the view that it is only observable *outcomes* that matter. The underlying preference - and, it should be said, value - structures are simply taken as given:

> The economist rarely examines the presuppositions of the models with which he works .... Individuals ... are presumed able to choose in accordance with their own preferences, whatever these may be, and the economist does not feel himself obliged to inquire deeply into the content of these preferences (the arguments in individuals' utility functions). (Buchanan 1987, p. 244)

On the other hand, because it is both institutionless and *intendedly* value-free,

> In ordinary or orthodox economics, no matter how simple or complex, analysis is concentrated on choices made *within* constraints that are, themselves, imposed exogenously to the person or persons charged with making the choice. The constraints that restrict the set of feasible choice options may be imposed by nature, by history, by a sequence of past choices, by other persons, by laws and institutional arrangements, or even by custom and convention. (Buchanan 1990, p. 379)

Their 'bounded rationality as ... theorists' (Smith 2003, p. 482) notwithstanding, economists must eschew theoretical and empirical 'tractability'. Simply stated, economists must abandon the teleological, consequence-based, procedurally-detached interpretation of economics and politics (Buchanan 1987, p. 244). Economists must recognize that, if each 'individual has a private, personal *history* [that] will have shaped both the preferences and the constraints that interact to determine choice behavior in any period t_o' (Brennan and Buchanan [1985] 2000, p. 79), the same individual 'at t_o, is one among many members of a given society, a community, that has its own history, as a political-collective entity, quite apart from the various collected histories of its individual members' (p. 84). Thus, if the *individual* has, *inter alia*, developed his own set of strictly personal, external and metapreferences, the 'society with a history' has developed 'historically determined constraints [which] may be descriptively summarized in the laws, institutions, customs, and traditions of the community, including the rules or institutions that define the means of making collective "choices"' (p. 84).

Granting all of this, the focus of interest shifts from choice *within* constraints to the *choice of* constraints. In an important sense the problem reduces to this: How might path-dependent, individuated preferences - whether strictly personal, external or meta - be reconciled with the path-dependent formal and informal institutions which characterize a 'society with a history'? As Brennan and Buchanan have suggested,

> At the most fundamental level, rules find their reason in the never-ending desire of people to live together in peace and harmony, without the continuing Hobbesian war of each against all. How can social order be established and preserved? All social science and philosophy must address this question, either directly or indirectly. ([1985] 2000, p. xv)

7.4 CONSTITUTIONAL POLITICAL ECONOMY: A CONSERVATIVE ECONOMICS

Inevitably, the question raised above - How can social order be established and preserved? - implicates moral and political philosophy. This, in turn, requires that I return to the three ideas which animate this chapter. The second, that economic theory must take explicit account of the path-dependency of persons' preference and value structures, and of the endogeneity of formal and informal institutions, is the subject matter of Section 7.3. This section concentrates on the first and third ideas. They are, respectively, that 'no economic theory makes proper sense until conjoined to some adequate political doctrine (a doctrine which defines the nature and rights of the social arrangement to be served)' (Scruton 2002, pp. 106-7), and that, given its Kantial roots, the focus of 'conservative' economics must be procedurally-based and consequence-detached.

In his Nobel lecture James Buchanan reminded his audience that, in 1949, he had

> called upon my fellow economists to postulate some model of the state, of politics, before proceeding to analyze the effects of alternative policy measures. I urged economists to look at the 'constitution of economic policy', to examine the rules, the constraints within which political agents act. Like Wicksell, my purpose was ultimately normative rather than antiseptically scientific. (1987, p. 243)

I emphasize, first, that the economist's theory of the state - social welfare theory - cannot answer the question, How can social order be established and preserved? Outcomes-based and procedurally-detached, the theory is both indeterminate (SS 4.7 and 4.9), and incapable of accommodating either the moral force of rights or any plausible theory of justice (S 4.10). That said, the 'area of inquiry' styled 'constitutional political economy' is animated by the following questions (Brennan and Buchanan [1985] 2000, p. 4):

> What advice can [economists] offer ... in our own societies, standing as we do with the benefits of cooperation and the prospects of conflict on either hand? What aspects of our social life should we discard? Where are the 'rules of social order' - institutional arrangements governing our interactions - that lead us to affect one another adversely? Where are there forces for harmony that can be mobilized? What rules - and what institutions - should we be struggling to preserve?[28]

Given this adumbration of the constitutional political economist's research agenda I suggest that his work is informed by the conservative's constitutive political position (CCPP). In this important sense, it is, in Scruton's words, 'conjoined to some adequate political doctrine'. Alternatively, to paraphrase James Buchanan, constitutional political economy (CPE) embraces a conservative 'model of the state, of politics'.[29]

To see this, consider first that both CPE and the CCPP are grounded in Kantian moral and political philosophy. Whereas CPE takes as a fundamental 'presupposition that persons must be evaluated as moral equals' (Brennan and Buchanan [1985] 2000, p. xviii), the Kantian two-person point of view is the foundation upon which the CCPP is built (S 5.5).[30]

Consider next that both CPE and the CCPP emphasize the role and importance of external or moralistic, altruistic and political preferences. From the perspective of the constitutional political economist,

> The scope for an individualistic, voluntaristic ethics must, of necessity, be progressively narrowed through time. As individuals, increasingly, find themselves caught in the large-number dilemma with respect to ethical choices, a possible logical explanation is provided for resort to political-governmental processes which can, effectively, change the rules and impose standards of conduct common to all individuals. In this respect, [CPE] analysis yields helpful insights concerning the 'legislation of morals'. (Buchanan [1965] 1999, p. 327)[31]

We have, then, that while the conservative rejects the liberal's natural rights against external preferences construal (SS 3.3 and 5.5), the constitutional political economist concludes that, given the large-number dilemma, 'the overwhelming probability would be that collectively enforced standards of conduct would be those desired for "others" by "some"' (p. 327). Simply stated, both CPE and the CCPP embrace the view that, at both the constitutional and the postconstitutional stage, explicit account must be taken of persons' moral and other external preferences.

If all of this is consistent with Kant's view that all political issues *are* moral issues (Kersting 1992, p. 343), it is also clear that both CPE and the CCPP share Kant's nonteleological moral and political philosophy (S 4.2).[32] Thus, for the constitutional political economist,

> there is no criterion through which policy may be directly evaluated. ... The focus of evaluative attention becomes the process itself, as contrasted with end-state or outcome patterns. ... The *constitution* of policy rather than policy itself becomes the relevant object for reform. (Buchanan 1987, p. 247)

The conservative shares the constitutional political economist's concern for 'process'. For the conservative, politics has no 'ruling purpose'. The imperative is not, and cannot be, the pursuit of 'good ends'. Rather, it is to ensure that the Moral Law and the other dimensions of moral argument and appraisal inform constitutional, statutory and common law (SS 3.4 and 5.5).

Finally, for the constitutional political economist, 'the public legitimacy of the government ... is a consequence of the distribution of decisions reached. ... politics that adhere to the [constitutional] generality constraint will be more consistent, less arbitrary, and less costly to run than politics that do not' (Buchanan and Congleton 1998, p. 142). As we have seen (S 5.5 and Chapter 6), this construction comports with the conservative view. Like the constitutional political economist, the conservative insists that intra- and intergenerational discrimination be constitutionally constrained.

In Section 1.1 I posed the question, Why *this* book? I suggested that the project is inspired by Professor Buchanan's 'frustration and irritation' - which he, correctly, believes I share - at 'some of our right-wing friends' attitudes toward the whole Rawlsian enterprise, as well as our left-wing adversaries' efforts to co-opt Rawls.'

I believe that the intervening pages have shown that the Kantian/Rawlsian framework has been misconstrued and misapplied: Whereas liberalism's constitutive and derivative political positions cannot be reconciled with Kant's two-person point of view, conservatism's political positions are *grounded* in this true, Kantian, construction. While, so far as I know, no explicit account has heretofore been taken of it, it is clear that the work of the constitutional political economist is informed by the same, true Kantian understanding of the self. It is in this sense that constitutional political economy *is* conservative economics.

I return, finally, to Roger Scruton's admonition that 'no economic theory makes proper sense until conjoined to some adequate political doctrine'. For constitutional political economics conservatism *is* that doctrine. It follows that the CPE enterprise cannot be 'co-opted' by its 'left-wing' adversaries. That said, given the problems which attend their transcendental, autonomous, first-person self construal,

> The best we can hope for ... is that liberals will begin to take their own ideology seriously, and so compromise with conservatism. They may call this compromise 'reflective equilibrium', as Rawls does, and thereby imagine that it is reasonable, in just the way that the first-person singular is always reasonable. (Scruton 2002, pp. 193-4)

That this will require embrace of Kant's two points of view is obvious. Were liberals to do this, they should not co-opt the Kantian/Rawlsian enterprise, they should have become conservatives - in the true, Kantian sense.

NOTES:
1.   Rabin and Thaler (2001) note that 'For nearly 50 years, economists have been fending off researchers who have identified clear departures from expected utility' (p. 230). Given its

'mathematical elegance, tractability and normative appeal', they conclude that 'the expected utility model clearly has "beautiful plumage"'. Yet, 'when the model is plainly wrong and frequently misleading, at some point economists must conclude that the plumage doesn't enter into it'. Granting this, they ask, 'What should expected utility theory be replaced with?' (p. 230). *Inter alia*, Richard Thaler (2000) has predicted that *'Homo Economicus* Will Begin Losing IQ, Reversing a 50-year Trend', and that *'Homo Economicus* Will Become More Emotional'.

2. At least in one account, 'economists ... simply stopped worrying about the realism of microassumptions (after Friedman 1953)' (Lewin 1996, p. 1319).

3. John Neville Keynes, cited by Friedman (1953, p. 3).

4. For a discussion of the conditions which must be satisfied if an assumption is to be 'realistic' see Wong (1973, pp. 317 and 320).

5. See also Wong (1973, p. 323).

6. Indeed, at least one economist has suggested that the scope of the phenomena which can be explained using the 'economics tool kit' is so broad that it 'suggests the possibility of unifying [all of] the social sciences in an economics-led hegemony' (Demsetz 1996 p. 1). Apparently, the hegemonic impulse has met with some success. See, for example, Baron and Hannan (1994) and Miller (1997).

7. A careful reading of Friedman's 'Methodology of Positive Economics' reveals a marked propensity to employ the word 'explain'. Indeed, he uses the word in what is clearly one of the most important passages in the essay:

> in general, the more significant the theory, the more unrealistic the assumptions. ... A hypothesis is important if it 'explains' much by little, that is, if it abstracts the common and crucial elements from the mass of complex and detailed circumstances surrounding the phenomena to be explained. ... To be important, therefore, a hypothesis must be descriptively false in its assumptions; it takes account of, and accounts for, none of the many other attendant circumstances, since its very success shows them to be irrelevant for the phenomena to be explained. (1953, pp. 14-15)

8. Heiner (1983) notes, for example, that 'optimization models have never been able to imply the Law of Demand' (1983, p. 561). See also Heiner's footnote number 4. Noting that violations of the axioms of revealed preferences can be ascribed to changes in tastes, Ekelund, Furubotn and Gramm suggest that 'Before observed consumer choices can be interpreted confidently it would seem essential to learn more about individual decision-making behavior under the conditions actually operative in the real world' (1972, p. 73). Caldwell (1983, p. 824) notes that the same problem attaches to empirical tests of the neoclassical maximization hypothesis. For alternative views, see Boland (1981) and Boland (1979).

9. In fact, 'as if' statements can serve neither to predict nor to explain. See Melitz (1965, p. 50). For a discussion of 'break downs' of the 'as if' principle, see DePalma, Myers and Papageorgiou (1994, pp. 433-4). For more on the 'as if' construal, see Russell and Thaler (1985, pp. 1080-81) and Mayer (1993, pp. 51-2).

10. See also Nagel (1963, pp. 214-15).

11. See also Leontief (1971).

12. Cox and Epstein (1989) suggest that the pattern of results of individual choice and market experiments

> could have two, quite different implications. On the one hand, it may turn out that we ... need to develop fundamentally different approaches to decision theory. ... On the other hand, it may be that our traditional models are incomplete but not fundamentally flawed. Recalling the traditional 'as if' interpretation of economic theory, it may be ... that the informational and disciplining properties of economic institutions cause real economic agents to learn to behave as if they are like our theoretical agents. (p. 423)

While I shall have more to say about this in Section 7.3, I note that the Nobel laureate experimental economist, Vernon Smith, suggests that 'the claim that it is "as if" agents had complete information, helps not a wit to understand the well-springs of behavior' (2003, p. 475).

13.   Douglass North summarizes the situation in this way: 'The rational-choice framework assumes that individuals know what is in their self-interest and act accordingly. ... but [this] is patently false in making choices under conditions of uncertainty' (1994, p. 362). Noting that 'a behavioral approach to economics has emerged in which assumptions are not sacroscant', Daniel Kahneman (2003) nevertheless concludes that

> conventional economic analysis is now being done with assumptions that are often much more psychologically plausible than was true in the past. However, the analytical methodology of economics is stable, and it will inevitably constrain the rapprochement between the disciplines. Whether or not psychologists find them odd and overly simple, the standard assumptions about the economic agent are in economic theory for a reason: they allow for tractable analysis. (pp. 165-6)

The 'standard assumptions' to which Kahneman refers are 'selfishness', 'rationality' and 'unchanging tastes and the carriers of utility'.

14.   The Nobel laureate Vernon Smith has indicated that 'I have no disagreement with Heiner's critique of classical preference theory, which is among the roots that should be reexamined' (1985, p. 271).

15.   For evidence in support of Heiner's theory of rule-governed behavior, see Wilde, LeBaron and Israelsen (1985) and Kaen and Rosenman (1986). For critiques of his approach, see Bookstaber and Langsam (1985) and Garrison (1985). See Heiner (1985b) for his Reply. For 'Further Modeling and Applications' of the theory, see Heiner (1985a). Finally, North suggests that, 'Ronald Heiner (1983), in a path-breaking article, not only made the connection between the mental capacities of humans and the external environment, but suggested the implications for arresting economic progress' (1994, p. 363, footnote 7).

16.   In this and similar situations,

> 'behavioral rules' ... arise because of uncertainty ... . Such uncertainty requires ... mechanisms that restrict the flexibility to choose potential actions, or which produce a selective alertness to information that might prompt particular actions to be chosen. These mechanisms simplify behavior to less-complex patterns, which are easier for an observer to recognize and predict. (Heiner 1983, p. 561)

17.   Indeed, Smith (2003, p. 465) notes that 'Historically, a recurrent theme in economics is that the values to which people respond are not confined to those one would expect based on the narrowly defined canons of rationality'. He cites, in particular, the work of Adam Smith (1759, 1776), David Hume ([1739] 1985, p. 507), Friedrich Hayek (1988, p. 18), and Herbert Simon (1996, p. 33).

18.   Significantly, Smith (2003, p. 467, footnote 9) emphasizes that he is 'Dissatisfied with the utilitarian approach because its predictions fail to account for the observed importance of instructions/procedures.' In his view,

> utilities can serve as intermediate placeholders for reciprocal trust, but, as surface indicators, serve poorly to generate new hypotheses designed to understand interactive processes. Good theory must be an engine for generating testable hypotheses, and utility theory runs out of fuel quickly. Utility values are seen as providing the ultimate 'given' data, and conversation stops.

19.   Robert H. Frank has proffered a model of the evolution of honesty (1987). *Inter alia*, he suggests that, whereas 'Modern economists regard behaviors arising from ... emotions as lying

outside the scope of our standard model', 'conscience and other moral sentiments also play a powerful role in the choices we make' (p. 603). While Harrington suggests that Frank's findings 'are based upon an implausible foundation' (1989, p. 588), he concludes that 'it should not be inferred ... that cooperation cannot be achieved via an evolutionary process. The fact is, it can'. He adds, moreover, that 'It is a weakness to the neoclassical approach that it has been unable to provide an adequate explanation for such behavior' (p. 592). In his 'Reply' to Harrington (1989), Frank insists that 'there is surely no doubt that many honest persons have managed to make their way into the population *somehow*' (p. 596).

20. 'Cartesian constructivism' refers here to the notion that 'all worthwhile social institutions were and should be created by conscious deductive processes of human reason' (Smith 2003, p. 467). In a more general sense, 'constructivism' refers to the orthodox, neoclassical model of constrained utility maximization.

21. Interestingly, the Nobel laureate econometrician, Trygve Haavelmo suggests that

> economic theory could make progress by an approach within the following framework. Starting with some existing society, we could conceive of it as a structure of rules and regulations within which the members of society have to operate. ... the results of the individuals in a society responding ... to the original rules ... have a feedback effect upon these rules themselves. (1997, p. 15)

22. Vernon Smith's analogue for Scruton's 'social knowledge' is 'social mind'. In his account, '"social mind" is born of the interaction among all individuals through the rules of institutions that have to date survived cultural selection processes' (2003, p. 500). Douglass North employs the characterization 'Collective learning - a term used by Friedrich Hayek - [which] consists of those experiences that have passed the slow test of time and are embodied in our language, institutions, technology, and ways of doing things' (1994, p. 364).

23. This, it should be noted, is also an implication of Heiner's competence-difficulty gap formulation (SS 4.6 and 7.3). In Heiner's account, 'legal and market institutions. ... evolve so as to provide predictable opportunity for mutual reciprocation situations; and so to reduce the scope and complexity of information that must be reliably interpreted for agents to benefit from these situations' (1983, p. 581). See also Heiner (1983, p. 586, especially footnote 64).

24. Drawing upon research in evolutionary psychology Cosmides and Tooby (1994) conclude that 'different "rules of the game" can be triggered in a lawful way by specific kinds of ecological variables' (p. 331). For a discussion, *inter alia*, of the role of biology in shaping altruistic and other preferences, see Robson (2001).

25. 'Constructivist tools' refers here to the standard, neoclassical model of constrained utility maximization. As Smith suggests, 'Expected utility theory is for teaching, ... but also for the constructivist modeling of consistent choice. It seems inadequate for the prediction, or the ecological understanding, of behavior. Its inadequacy for prediction has been plainly emphasized in the many contributions of Amos Tversky and Daniel Kahneman' (2003, p. 469, footnote 15). For more on the 'system [that] governs emotional responses that lead a person to discover for himself behavioral rules of the family, tribe, or other organizations' see Wilde, LeBaron and Israelsen (1985, p. 405).

26. Smith (2003, p. 469) summarizes the situation this way: 'Having sharpened our understanding on Cartesian complete information parables [economists] carry the tools into the world for application without all the necessary caveats that reflect the tractability constraints imposed by our bounded professional cognitive capacities as theorists'.

27. For more on 'the rules of reciprocity that people learn in everyday life', the culture-dependent nature of 'rules, expectations or notions of fairness' and the 'genetic and adaptive underpinnings for the propensity to cooperate based on the development and growth of social norms', see Camerer and Thaler (1995), Henrich (2000), Ostrom (2000) and Fehr and Gächter (2000). For more on the notion that 'institutions matter', see Smith (1989). Interestingly, Smith notes that 'In economics the tendency of theory to lag behind observation seems to be endemic, and, as theorists, few of us consider this to be a "terrible state". But as noted by Lakatos ... "where

theory lags behind the facts, we are dealing with miserable degenerating research programmes"' (p. 168).

28. As we have seen (S 6.3) a central proposition of constitutional political economy is that certain government activities must be constitutionally constrained. Particular emphasis is placed upon a generality or impartiality constraint (SS 6.3, 6.4, 6.5 and 6.6). Interestingly, Ronald Heiner suggests that, in the presence of a competence-difficulty gap (SS 4.6 and 7.3), 'society will benefit by appropriately limiting the scope and complexity of government behavior'. To the question, 'how is such limitation to arise?' he suggests that 'It is here that we enter the area of constitutionalism, defined broadly as the design of rule-mechanisms to restrict the flexibility of government'. He adds, moreover, that 'The writings of seventeenth- and eighteenth-century political philosophers and statesmen were primarily concerned with these issues' (1983, p. 586).

29. It should be clear that the constitutional political economist's enterprise is incommensurable with 'scientific', intendedly value-free economics. From the conservative's perspective this is essential:

> the purely scientific economist might have to see civil society as a corpse, moving in obedience to scientific laws which can be formulated without reference to the conceptions, values and feelings through which people understand themselves as political beings. The only result of that scientific process would be to render politics incomprehensible, to retreat from direct involvement in it, and to cease to want either to belong or not to belong to the social arrangement by which one is surrounded. (Scruton 2002, pp. 91-2)

For more on the 'scientific' economist's instrumentalist methodology, see Scruton (1994, especially p. 191).

30. The idea of ordinary conscience - that the agent's action is, or should be, both constrained and animated by the Moral Law, by the ethic of virtue, by sympathy and by piety - is derivative of Kant's two points of view and is central to the conservative's constitutive political position (S 5.4).

31. Buchanan's hypothesis is that 'the size of the group within which [an individual] consciously interacts is a critical determinant' of the individual's choice among ethical rules ([1965] 1999, p. 311). He assumes, for expository purposes, that an individual can 'adopt a rule, which we shall call "the moral law", or he can adopt a rule which, loosely, we shall call "the private maxim"' (p. 313). While choice of the former means that he will 'not act in ways other than those which allow his ... action to be universalized, regardless of the consequences', choice of the second means that he 'retains freedom to act on the basis of expedient considerations' (p. 313). On the presumption that an individual's 'own choice of a rule, and subsequent adherence to it, will to some considerable extent influence the similar choices to be made and followed [by others]' (p. 319), Buchanan concludes that

> for any given individual who may ... follow ... the rule of moral law in his small-group interactions, there is some increase in group size that will cause him to modify his ethical rule and become a private maximizer. (p. 322)

The 'large-number dilemma' to which Buchanan refers is contemplated by Heiner's (1983) competence-difficulty gap analysis. As Wilde, LeBaron and Israelsen suggest, 'That institutions must evolve which enable each agent in the society to know less and less about the behavior of other agents, and about the complex interdependencies generated by their interactions, is an implication of Heiner's theory' (1985, p. 406).

32. As has been emphasized, in the case of teleological theories, 'the good is defined independently from the right, and then the right is defined as that which maximizes the good' (Rawls 1971, p. 24).

8. A Postscript on Law

8.1 THE CHOICE OF CONSTRAINTS PROBLEM: A REPRISE

The discussion in SS 7.3 and 7.4 suggests, *inter alia*, that constitutional political economy (CPE) *is* conservative economics. Among the elements of congruence between CPE and the conservative's constitutive political position (CCPP) is the idea that custom, traditions, and social and moral behavioral norms should, and do, inform constitutional, statutory and common law. Equally important, the endogeneity of formal institutions, of which law is among the most important, implicates the choice of con- straints problem; a problem which, in turn, is central to the CPE enterprise. I emphasize, again, that the problem reduces to this: How might path- dependent, individuated, strictly personal, external and metapreferences be reconciled with the path-dependent formal and informal institutions which characterize a 'society with a history'?

If this problem - and its solution - finds expression in the CCPP and, *pari passu*, in the work of the constitutional political economist, it animates discussion in the contemporary philosophy of law. At least in one account, 'The issue which stands behind nearly every controversy in contemporary legal theory is the problem of how law is to be understood in relation to moral values' (Tebbit 2000, p.3).

With this as background, the balance of this chapter concentrates on an analysis of three competing theories of law, and on an adumbration of what I shall characterize as a conservative theory of law. A recurring theme, informed by the argument developed in preceding chapters, is that law and morality are inexorably intertwined, and that a proper understanding of that relationship is central to the solution of the choice of constraints problem.

8.2 THREE THEORIES OF LAW: AN OVERVIEW

Given their prominence, interest centers on three, competing legal theories. I consider first what Ronald Dworkin (1978) has called, 'the ruling theory of law'.[1] Broadly speaking, legal positivism - the conceptual part of the theory - may be regarded as the analogue for the logical positivism which informs the economist's 'scientific', intendedly value-free social welfare theory (S 4.5). Derivative of Jeremy Bentham's theory of law, the ruling theory is characterized by a 'separation thesis'.[2] In this account, the conceptual part of the theory insists that concepts such as 'legality', 'legal validity' and 'legal system' must exclude consideration of moral content, moral validity or moral appraisal (Tebbit 2000, p. 36). For its part, the normative part of the ruling theory supposes that 'legal institutions compose a system whose overall goal is the promotion of the highest average welfare among [the] individuals' who make up a community (Dworkin 1978, p. ix). As might be expected, given its Benthamite origins and its empirical, anti-metaphysical orientation, the ruling theory rejects the idea of natural rights (Dworkin 1978, p. xi).

The Chicago approach deploys social welfare theory's first and second fundamental welfare theorems (S 4.5) in constructing a positive and normative approach to law and economics. On the presumption that judges act 'as if' they are trying to maximize society's wealth, the former contemplates determining whether prevailing common law doctrines comport with the strictures of first-best Paretian optimality or economic efficiency, while the latter focuses on the determination of efficient legal rules to guide legislative and judicial decision making (Mercuro and Medema 1997, p. 61). Moreover, insofar as a legal change produces winners and losers, the theory invokes the compensation principle, or Kaldor-Hicks efficiency.[3] In either case, the desideratum is societal 'wealth maximization' (p. 19). Finally, whereas there is a view that 'there are questions of fairness as between the parties [in litigation] that are not answerable in economic terms' (Epstein 1973, p. 152), the Chicago approach suggests that if a legal standard 'appears to impose avoidable costs on society' the burden is on its authors to justify the standard (Mercuro and Medema 1997, p. 73).

Ronald Dworkin's 'liberal theory of law' rejects the separation thesis and embraces the view - antithetical to the ruling theory - that individuals have natural rights. In his account, lawyers and judges appeal not only to black letter rules, but also to legal principles 'like, for example, the principle that no man may profit from his own wrong' (1978, p. 46). Dworkin insists that judges have a duty to be guided both by the requirement of 'best fit' with all relevant legal precedent, and by the criterion of 'best light'; a duty, that is, to find interpretations of legal precedents which provide the best political reading of the received, common law (Tebbit 2000, p. 59). It is in this sense that his mythical, omniscient judge Hercules (Dworkin 1978, pp. 105-30) is said to be constrained, *inter alia*, by moral objectivism; by the presumption that 'there can be only one morally sound interpretation of precedent' (Tebbit 2000, p. 59). Granting all of this, no distinction can be made between legal and moral standards: 'Political rights are creatures of both history and morality: what an individual is entitled to have, in civil society, depends upon both the practice and the justice of its political institutions' (Dworkin 1978, p. 87). Justice, in turn, rests on the Kantian/Rawlsian assumption 'of a natural right of all men and women to equality of concern and respect' (p. 182). As we have seen, this idea is the basis of Dworkin's rights as non-absolute trumps against external preferences construal.

8.3 THE RULING THEORY OF LAW

The conceptual part of the ruling theory, legal positivism, insists upon a 'separation' between law and morality. This suggests, *inter alia*, that, in their jurisprudential role, judges can, and do, conduct intendedly value-free analysis.

While much can be said about this, the essential point is that appeal to 'black letter rules of law' cannot proceed *in vacuo*. Judges, like all agents, are not, and cannot be, transcendental, autonomous selves. Agency requires a motive to act and this, in turn, requires immersion in contingent, empirical conditions. For their part, empirical conditions contemplate all manner of path-dependent phenomena, including both formal and informal institutions. While the former includes constitutional, statutory and common law, the latter contemplates the Moral Law, the ethic of virtue, sympathy and piety - the determinants of 'ordinary conscience' (S 5.4).

Consider first that the American legal and constitutional tradition is predicated on the idea that similar cases ought to be treated similarly. Clearly derivative of the Kantian Moral Law, this conception is a reflection of the idealized rule of law (S 6.3). In effect, 'the conception of formal justice, the regular and impartial administration of public rules, becomes the rule of law when applied to the legal system' (Rawls 1971, p. 235). Given that American jurisprudence is animated by this Kantian idea, legal positivism's insistence that law and morality can be 'separated' denies objective features of observable reality.[4]

If the Moral Law informs American jurisprudence, so *must* the other dimensions of moral argument and appraisal. Following Kant ([1785] 1988, p. 87), the 'web of attachments'-animated vision of the good 'that leads people to see the world in terms of value' (Scruton 2002, p. 192) imbues *all* persons with 'common intuitions of morality' (Scruton 1982, p.

58). Thus, in 'hard cases' in which, *inter alia*, rights and duties conflict, judges, like all persons, may be expected to address the claims of virtue; to ask the question, 'Would a virtuous person perform the action(s) in question?'. Then 'when all requirements of right and virtue have been met, [the judge] can respond to the call of sympathy', a call which may, in turn, 'compete with piety'. Whatever the outcome of this evaluative process, the judge, like all agents, will have engaged in the practice of ordinary conscience (Scruton 1996, pp. 125-6).[5] While this characterization of the process of moral appraisal contrasts with the Chicago Approach - which imagines that judges' utility is a function of income, leisure and judicial voting (Mercuro and Medema 1997, p. 65) - it seems broadly to comport with Dworkin's understanding of the immanence of moral appraisal in legislators' and judges' thinking: What is required, Dworkin insists, is a 'scheme of civil rights' which will, antecedently, *prohibit* judicial and other consideration of political, altruistic and moralistic preferences.

Because, in practice, judges invoke rules and moral standards or 'principles', law and morality are inseparably intertwined. It follows, *pari passu*, that the conceptual part of the ruling theory of law, legal positivism, is fundamentally misleading. Equally important, the inseparability of law and morality suggests that the 'sphere of law' may legitimately contemplate 'all that matters to social continuity, all that can be taken as standing in need of state protection' (Scruton 2002, p. 68). On this logic, external preferences 'count', and laws may legitimately restrict 'what some would call the "freedom" of the citizen' (p. 70).

If the conceptual part of the ruling theory denies objective features of observable reality, its normative part is logically incoherent. Given the presumption that 'legal institutions compose a system whose overall goal is the promotion of the highest average welfare among ... individuals' (Dworkin 1978, p. ix), the latter implicitly endorses a form of rule utilitarianism. Whether in preference or welfare form, rule utilitarianism 'limits the application of the standard of utility to rules or social institutions and requires compliance with rules that are certified as having the requisite utilitarian justification' (Lyons 1982, p. 128). In effect, the obligation to obey legal (and other) rules is derived from 'criteria drawn from consequentialist arguments about the likely outcomes of specific acts of disobedience or a general rejection of the authority of the law' (Tebbit 2000, p. 79). The problem is that 'evaluation of conduct from a utilitarian standpoint is dominated by direct utilitarian arguments and therefore ignores the moral force of justified legal rights' (Lyons 1982, p. 113).

Stated differently, 'there is no deep compatibility between the doctrine of utility and the concept of a right' (Tebbit, 2000, p. 109). It follows that the normative part of the ruling theory cannot, logically, generate an obligation to obey the law.

8.4 THE CHICAGO APPROACH TO LAW AND ECONOMICS

Because it is grounded in utilitarian social welfare theory the Chicago approach to law and economics is subject to the same debility. In their effort to deploy the first and second fundamental welfare theorems, proponents of the Chicago approach take no explicit account of the irreconcilability of goal- and right-based moral theories (SS 4.3 and 4.8). Granting this, both social welfare theorists and proponents of the Chicago approach to law and economics face a conundrum: Either they must argue that the legal rights which they regard as instrumentally important are morally exigent in themselves, and reject the efficient standard, or they must embrace the efficiency standard and deny the moral force of rights.

If the 'rights problem' calls into question the efficacy of the Chicago approach, so too does the indeterminancy of the efficiency standard (S 4.7). It follows that judicial decisions, and changes in statutory law informed by the first and second fundamental welfare theorems, must be regarded as *ad hoc*.[6] The logic of both positive and normative law and economics is therefore undermined.[7]

8.5 THE LIBERAL THEORY OF LAW

Ronald Dworkin's liberal theory of law rejects the separation thesis. With this I agree. But the theory also embraces a view - antithetical to the ruling theory, but problematic in its own right - that individuals have natural rights against others' external preferences (S 3.3).

The problems with this enterprise has been discussed at length. While the argument need not be reprised, the problem of immediate interest is that, while the idealized rule of law *is* an extension of the Moral Law, the liberal's interpretation of 'the property of the will to be a law to itself' goes too far. Its insistence that government must be 'neutral on what might be called the question of the good life' has as its corollary a tolerance imperative (S 1.6). The imperative, in short, is to be non-judgmental; to give 'moral and political space' to the transcendental, autonomous self. Indeed, the liberal theory of law insists that individuals have rights which are antecedent to civil society. In this account, individuals have 'background rights, which are [political] rights that hold in an abstract way against decisions taken by the community or the society as a whole' (Dworkin 1978, p.xii). This 'rights conception' of the rule of law

> assumes that citizens have moral rights and duties with respect to one another, and political rights against the state as a whole. It insists that these moral and political rights be recognized in positive law, so that they may be enforced *upon the demand of individual citizens* through courts or other judicial institutions of the familiar type, so far as this is practicable. The rule of law on this conception is the ideal rule of law by an accurate public conception of individual rights. (Dworkin 1985, pp. 11-2)

These ideas find expression in the conclusions reached by Dworkin's 'lawyer of superhuman skill, learning, patience and acumen', Judge Hercules (1978, p. 105):

> Hercules' first conclusion, that the gravitational force of a precedent is defined by the arguments of principle that support the precedent, suggests a second. Since judicial practice in his community assumes that earlier cases have a *general* gravitational force, then he can justify that judicial practice only *by supposing that the rights thesis holds in his community.* (p. 150) (emphasis mine)

The 'rights thesis', which is intended to provide 'an account of the interaction of personal and institutional morality', holds that 'judicial decisions enforce existing political rights' (p. 87). In Dworkin's account,

> If the thesis holds, then institutional history acts not as a constraint on the political judgment of judges but as an ingredient of that judgment, because institutional history is part of the background that any plausible judgment about the rights of an individual must accommodate. Political rights are creatures of both history and morality. (p. 87)

Granting this, 'Judges should enforce only political convictions that they believe, in good faith, can figure in a coherent general interpretation of the legal and political culture of the community' (Dworkin 1985, p. 2).

On the *presumption* that he 'suppose[s] that the rights thesis holds in his community', it follows that a judge 'supposes that citizens have moral rights - that is, rights other than and prior to those given by positive enactment' (p. 13). It is in this sense that judicial decisions must enforce 'existing' background or antecedent rights; rights which exist independently of the customs, traditions and behavioral and moral norms that define a society's 'social traditions and informal rules' (S 7.3).[8]

Problems with this construction abound. First, there can be no presumption that the 'rights thesis holds in [a judge's] community'. It is not at all clear that persons whose utility functions include interpersonal effects *necessarily* endorse the idea that others possess antecedent, 'background' rights against external preferences. In any case, it *is* clear that persons' political, altruistic and moralistic preferences both affect, and are affected by, the customs and traditions that constitute 'social knowledge' and shape law (S 7.3). Second, the rights as trumps against external preferences construal is rooted in a truncated vision of the transcendental, autonomous self (SS 1.4 and 3.2). Finally, and relatedly, neither the justification of, nor respect for, the rights which the theory seeks to protect can be generated by appeal to the transcendental, autonomous self (S 3.3). These and other considerations inform the conservative theory of law.

8.6 THE CONSERVATIVE THEORY OF LAW

Given its embrace of the Kantian two-person perspective, the conservative theory of law rejects both the separation thesis (S 8.3) and the consequence-based, procedurally-detached Chicago approach to law and economics (S 8.4). While it shares with its liberal counterpart the view that 'political rights are creatures of both history and morality' (S 8.2), there are fundamental differences.

I emphasize, first, that whereas the liberal theory asserts that individuals have natural or background rights against the state and each other (SS 1.3, 1.4 and 8.5), the conservative theory insists that rights are neither antecedent to civil society (S 3.3), nor a source of moral license.

Informed, as it must be, by the conservative's constitutive political position (S 5.5), the conservative theory of law sees individuals not as transcendental, autonomous selves, but rather as individuals whose 'web of attachments' requires that they 'see themselves as the inheritors, not the creators of the order in which they participate, so that they may derive from it ... the conceptions and values which determine self-identity' (Scruton 2002, p. 60). Central to this construction is the notion that 'self-identity' is defined in the Kantian two-person sense (S 3.2). On the one hand, examples of honesty, steadfastness, sympathy and benevolence encourage the individual to imagine himself to be a better person and, *pari passu*, to treat others as ends rather than as means (Kant [1785] 1988, p. 87). On the other hand, 'self-identity' contemplates a sense of allegiance such that, while individuals do 'exist and act as autonomous beings', they do so 'only because they can first identify themselves as something greater - as members of a society, group, class, state, or nation' (Scruton 2002, p. 24).

In this account, 'personal freedom' is 'not the precondition but the consequence of an accepted social arrangement' (2002, p. 8). Thus, while 'it is the individual's responsibility to win whatever freedom of speech, conscience and assembly he may' (p. 8), 'if individuality threatens allegiance - as it must do in a society where individuality seeks to realize itself in opposition to the institutions from which it grows - then the civil order is threatened too' (p. 25). Granting this,

> The authority of the law, however filtered through the apparatus of the state, depends upon the sense of social cohesion. And no law which tries to transcend that sense will ever have the firm allegiance of the citizens. Likewise, any area of social life which is vital either to the strength of the social bond, or to the social image of its participants, will be one into which the law may legitimately intrude. (Scruton 2002, p. 73)

Whereas the liberal theory, following Mill (S 1.3), emphasizes individuality, perfectibility, and freedom from the 'despotism of custom', the conservative theory of law insists that custom, tradition, and the other elements of social knowledge (S 7.3) must *inform* the law. Thus, if liberalism and, *pari passu*, the liberal theory of law seek to '[extend] the sphere of choice into those realms where traditionally people have sought not permission but constraint' (Scruton 2002, p. 74), the conservative theory asserts that

> To the extent that, one by one, customs, manners, morals, education, labour and rest are 'liberated' from its jurisdiction, so too does the sense of their social validity suffer a decline, as citizens find the gulf widening between their customs and their form of life, and the law which supposedly protects them. (pp. 74-5)

The contours of liberal and conservative legal thinking can be brought into sharper relief. In *Lawrence et al. v. Texas* (539 U.S. (2003)), the majority Opinion of the Supreme Court of the United States deploys the logic of the liberal theory of law. In sharp contrast, Justice Scalia's Dissent invokes the conservative theory.

The Opinion of the Court, written by Justice Kennedy, held that a Texas statute making it a crime for two persons of the same sex to engage in certain intimate sexual conduct violates the Due Process Clause of the Fourteenth Amendment to the United States Constitution.[9] At page one of the Opinion Justice Kennedy asserts that

Freedom extends beyond spatial bounds. Liberty presumes an *autonomy of self* that includes freedom of thought, belief, expression, and certain intimate conduct. The instant case involves liberty of the person both in its spatial and more *transcendental* dimensions. (emphasis mine)

Given this predicate, Justice Kennedy writes that 'We conclude the case should be resolved by determining whether the petitioners were free as adults to engage in the private conduct in the exercise of their liberty under the Due Process Clause of the Fourteenth Amendment' (p. 3).

Finally, in reaching the majority opinion that the Texas statute is unconstitutional, Justice Kennedy cites Justice Stevens' dissenting opinion in an earlier case (*Bowers v. Hardwick*, 478 US 186 (1986)):

Our prior cases make two propositions abundantly clear. First, the fact that the governing majority in a State has traditionally viewed a particular practice as immoral is not a sufficient reason for upholding a law prohibiting the practice; neither history nor tradition could save a law prohibiting miscegenation from constitutional attack. Second, individual decisions by married persons, concerning the intimacies of their physical relationship ... are a form of 'liberty' protected by the Due Process Clause. ... Moreover, this protection extends to intimate choices by unmarried as well as married persons.[10]

Justice Kennedy concludes, for the majority, that 'JUSTICE STEVENS' analysis, in our view, should have been controlling in *Bowers* and should control here' (539 US (2003), p. 17).

I note, first, that Justice Kennedy's invocation of the 'autonomy of self .... both in its spatial and more transcendental dimensions' is congruent with liberalism's constitutive political position (SS 1.3 and1.4). Second, the view that 'neither history nor tradition could save a law prohibiting miscegenation from constitutional attack' is consistent with liberalism's rights as trumps against external preferences construal:

I argue ... against counting external preferences, whether malevolent or altruistic, good or bad, in some utilitarian justification for a political decision. ... The fact that the majority thinks that homosexuality is immoral or that cruelty to children is wrong should not, in my view, count as an argument for anything, although, of course, the different fact that cruelty harms children does count very much. (Dworkin 1978, p. 358)

For Justice Scalia, joined in dissent by Justices Rehnquist and Thomas, the Opinion's logic is unacceptable. He notes, *inter alia*, that 'nowhere does the Court's opinion declare that homosexual sodomy is a "fundamental right" under the Due Process Clause; nor does it subject the Texas law to the standard of review that would be appropriate (strict scrutiny) if homosexual sodomy *were* a "fundamental right"' (539 U.S. (2003), pp. 1-2). Significantly, Justice Scalia argues that

> We have held repeatedly, in cases the Court today does not overrule, that *only* fundamental rights qualify for ... so-called 'heightened scrutiny' - that is, rights which are 'deeply rooted in this Nation's history and tradition' ... fundamental liberty interests must be 'so rooted in the traditions and conscience of our people as to be ranked as fundamental ... .' (Fourteenth Amendment protects 'those privileges *long recognized at common law* as essential to the orderly pursuit of happiness by free men' (emphasis added)). All other liberty interests may be abridged or abrogated pursuant to a validly enacted state law if that law is rationally related to a legitimate state interest. (pp. 8-9)

If the view that 'fundamental liberty interests' must be 'rooted in the traditions and conscience of our people' is a transparently conservative conception, so too is Justice Scalia's attack on the Court's 'holding that there is no rational basis for the law here under attack':

> This proposition is so out of accord with our jurisprudence - indeed, with the jurisprudence of *any* society we know - that it requires little discussion. The Texas statute undeniably seeks to further the belief of its citizens that certain forms of sexual behavior are 'immoral and unacceptable'. ... Bowers held that this *was* a legitimate state interest. ... The Court embraces instead JUSTICE STEVENS' declaration in his *Bowers* dissent, that 'the fact that the governing majority in a State has traditionally viewed a particular practice as immoral is not a sufficient reason for upholding a law prohibiting the practice'. ... This effectively decrees the end of all morals legislation. (pp. 14-15)

Finally, Justice Scalia articulates the conservative view that an independent judiciary must be a *conservative* force, respecting the social knowledge embodied in custom, tradition and the common law while, at the same time, acknowledging 'the individual's responsibility to win whatever freedom ... he may' (Scruton 2002, p. 8):

> Let me be clear that I have nothing against homosexuals, or any other group, promoting their agenda through normal democratic means. Social perceptions of sexual and other morality change over time, and every group has the right to persuade its fellow citizens that its view of such matters is the best. ... But persuading one's fellow citizens is one thing, and imposing one's view in absence of democratic majority will is something else. I would no more *require* a State to criminalize homosexual acts ... than I would *forbid* it to do so. (p. 19)

I emphasize, again, that my purpose in adumbrating the essential elements of *Lawrence v. Texas* is unexceptionable. I seek only to provide a 'bright line' illustration of the liberal and conservative theories of law 'at work'. That said, I embrace the conservative's view that the liberal's transcendental, autonomous self conception must be rejected; that 'fundamental liberty interests' are 'rooted in the traditions and conscience of [a] people', and that morality is a 'legitimate state interest'. It could not be otherwise. A prior commitment to Kantian moral philosophy has as it corollary a commitment to Kant's two-person point of view. If, as Kant suggests, it is 'examples of honesty of purpose, of steadfastness in following good maxims, of sympathy and general benevolence' that cultivate the Moral Law, it is also true that 'background' rights against moralistic external preferences corrode the conscience which the liberal seeks to nurture.

Transcendental autonomy, moral pluralism and institutional skepticism are surely not the answer to Professor Buchanan's question, 'How can social order be established and preserved?':

> It there is no point at which the liberal can rest with what is given, and find value immanent in the world, without recourse to transcendental illusions, then the liberal will never rest - not, at least, until he has torn down every law and every institution with his exterminating 'why?'. He who shifts the onus, will have to shift everything; he will confront, then, a world bereft of social artifacts, principal among which is morality itself. (Scruton 2002, p. 192)

If onus shifting and individuated moral codes are not the answer to Buchanan's question, then surely this is: Both ordinary conscience and social knowledge must find expression in constitutional, statutory and common law.

NOTES

1. In one account, Dworkin 'is widely considered the most important American legal philosopher of our time' (Farber and Sherry 2002, p. 122).
2. Ronald Dworkin puts the matter succinctly: 'positivism ... insists that law and morals are made wholly distinct by semantic rules everyone accepts for "using law"' (1986, p. 98). See also Dworkin (1985, pp. 13-6).
3. Kaldor-Hicks efficiency 'is also suggestively called potential Pareto efficiency. The winners could compensate the losers, but need not (not always, anyway)' (Posner 1986, p. 13).
4. If the Moral Law constitutes the external morality of law, its internal morality 'provides a basis for establishing a necessary connection between law and substantive morality' (Ten 1995, p. 397).
5. See also Section 5.4.
6. David Friedman (2000) lists four limitations of the efficiency criterion for judging legal rules. He acknowledges that 'If [its proponents] were claiming that economic efficiency was a perfect

criterion ... these would be serious, probably fatal, objections to the claim'. That said, he asserts that 'They are less serious if our claim is only that it is the best criterion available' (p. 22).

7. Dworkin agrees that 'Economic analysis of law is a descriptive and a normative theory' (1985, p. 263). That said, he asks, 'Does the failure of the normative limb impair the descriptive limb?' (p. 263). He rejects the 'normative limb' on the plausible grounds that the wealth maximization hypothesis 'seems weak, and is far from demonstrated' (p. 263). For its part, he finds the 'descriptive claims of economic analysis ... [to be] radically incomplete' (p. 264). Interestingly, his rejection of the 'descriptive limb' is predicated on the idea that economists take insufficient account of 'nonmotivational' explanations of human behavior. He cites, in particular, 'genetic or chemical or neurological accounts of either reflex or reflective behavior' (p. 263). This, it seems to me, is consistent with the argument developed in Section 7.3.

8. In this view, 'hard cases - that is, cases in which no explicit rule in the rule book firmly decides the case either way' (Dworkin 1985, p. 13) - must be decided on the basis of the 'best fit' of the background moral rights of the parties (pp. 16-17). Ideally, these background rights 'will be enforced in spite of the fact that no Parliament had the time or the will to enforce them' (p. 27).

9. Section 1. of the Fourteenth Amendment to the Constitution of the United States reads, in part, 'nor shall any State deprive any person of life, liberty, or property, without due process of law; nor deny to any person within its jurisdiction the equal protection of laws'. Justice O'Connor, concurring in the Court's judgment, writes that 'The Texas statute makes homosexuals unequal in the eyes of the law by making particular conduct - and only that conduct - subject to criminal sanction' (539 US (2003), p. 3).

10. Cited at 539 US (2003), p. 17.

References

Aaron, H.J. (1994), 'Public policy, values, and consequences', *Journal of Economic Perspectives*, 8(2), 3-21.

Aarsleff, Hans (1994), 'Locke's influence', in Vere Chappell (ed.), *The Cambridge Companion to Locke*, Cambridge: Cambridge University Press, pp. 252-89.

Almond, B. (1993), 'Rights', in Peter Singer (ed.), *A Companion to Ethics*, Cambridge, MA: Blackwell Publishers, Ltd., pp. 259-69.

Arrow, K.J. (1951), *Social Choice and Individual Value*, New Haven: Yale University Press.

Ashcraft, R. (1994), 'Locke's political philosophy', in Vere Chappell (ed.), *The Cambridge Companion to Locke*, Cambridge: Cambridge University Press, pp. 226-51.

Baron, J.N. and M.T. Hannan (1994), 'The impact of economics on contemporary sociology', *Journal of Economic Literature*, 32(3), 1111-46.

Barry, Brian (1989), *Theories of Justice*, Berkeley: University of California Press.

Black, Duncan (1958), *Theory of Committees and Elections*, Cambridge: Cambridge University Press.

Boland, L.A. (1979), 'A critique of Friedman's critics', *Journal of Economic Literature*, 17(2), 503-22.

Boland, L.A. (1981), 'On the futility of criticizing the neoclassical maximization hypothesis', *American Economic Review*, 71(5), 1031-6.

Bolton, G.E. and A. Ockenfels (2000), 'ERC: A theory of equity, reciprocity, and competition', *American Economic Review*, 90(1), 166-93.

Bookstaber, R. and J. Langsam (1985), 'Predictable behavior: Comment', *American Economic Review*, 75(3), 571-5.

Bovard, James (1995), *Lost Rights: The Destruction of American Liberty*, New York: St. Martin's Griffin.

Bovard, James (1999), *Freedom in Chains: The Rise of the State and the Demise of the Citizen*, New York: St. Martin's Press.

Brennan, Geoffrey (1995), 'The contribution of economics', in Robert E. Goodin and Philip Pettit (eds), *A Companion to Contemporary Political Philosophy*, Cambridge, MA: Blackwell Publishers, Ltd., pp. 123-56.

Brennan, Geoffrey and James M. Buchanan (1985), *The Reason of Rules: Constitutional Political Economy*, reprinted in Geoffrey Brennan, Hartmut Kliemt and Robert D. Tollison (eds) (2000), *The Collected Works of James M. Buchanan*, vol. 10, Indianapolis: Liberty Fund.

Buchanan, J. M. (1954), 'Social choice, democracy, and free markets', *Journal of Political Economy*, 62, 114-23.

Buchanan, James M. (1959), 'Positive economics, welfare economics, and political economy', in Geoffrey Brennan, Hartmut Kliemt and Robert D. Tollison (eds) (1999), *The Collected Works of James M. Buchanan*, vol. 1, Indianapolis: Liberty Fund, pp. 191-209.

Buchanan, James M. (1962), 'Politics, policy and the Pigovian margins', in Geoffrey Brennan, Hartmut Kliemt and Robert D. Tollison (eds) (1999), *The Collected Works of James M. Buchanan*, vol.1, Indianapolis: Liberty Fund, pp. 60-74.

Buchanan, James M. (1965), 'Ethical rules, expected values, and large numbers', in Geoffrey Brennan, Hartmut Kliemt and Robert D. Tollison (eds) (1999), *The Collected Works of James M. Buchanan*, vol. 1, Indianapolis: Liberty Fund, pp. 311-28.

Buchanan, James M. (1967), *Public Finance in Democratic Process: Fiscal Institutions and Individual Choice*, reprinted in Geoffrey Brennan, Hartmut Kliemt and Robert D. Tollison (eds) (1999), *The Collected Works of James M. Buchanan*, vol. 4, Indianapolis: Liberty Fund.

Buchanan, James M. (1968), *The Demand and Supply of Public Goods*, reprinted in Geoffrey Brennan, Hartmut Kliemt and Robert D. Tollison (eds) (1999), *The Collected Works of James M. Buchanan*, vol. 5, Indianapolis: Liberty Fund.

Buchanan, James M. (1975), *The Limits of Liberty: Between Anarchy and Leviathan*, reprinted in Geoffrey Brennan, Hartmut Kliemt and Robert D. Tollison (eds) (2000), *The Collected Works of James M. Buchanan*, vol. 7, Indianapolis: Liberty Fund.

Buchanan, James M. (1979), *What Should Economists Do?*, Indianapolis: The Liberty Fund.

Buchanan, James M. (1986), *Liberty, Market and State: Political Economy in the 1980s*, New York: New York University Press

Buchanan, James M. (1987), 'The constitution of economic policy', *American Economic Review*, 77(3), 243-50.

Buchanan, James M. (1989), 'The ethics of constitutional order', in Geoffrey Brennan, Hartmut Kliemt and Robert D. Tollison (eds) (1999), *The Collected Works of James M. Buchanan*, vol. 1, Indianapolis: Liberty Fund, pp. 368-73.

Buchanan, James M. (1990), 'The domain of constitutional economics', in Geoffrey Brennan, Hartmut Kliemt and Robert D. Tollison (eds) (1999), *The Collected Works of James M. Buchanan*, vol. 1, Indianapolis: Liberty Fund, pp. 377-95.

Buchanan, James M. (1991), *The Economics and the Ethics of Constitutional Order*, Ann Arbor: University of Michigan Press.

Buchanan, J. M. (1994a), 'Choosing what to choose', *Journal of Institutional and Theoretical Economics*, 150(1), 123-35.

Buchanan, James M. (1994b), *Ethics and Economic Progress*, Norman: University of Oklahoma Press.

Buchanan, James M. and Roger D. Congleton (1998), *Politics by Principle not Interest: Towards Nondiscriminatory Democracy*, Cambridge: Cambridge University Press.

Buchanan, James M. and Gordon Tullock (1962), *The Calculus of Consent: Logical Foundations of Constitutional Democracy*, Ann Arbor: University of Michigan Press.

Caldwell, B.J. (1983), 'The neoclassical maximization hypothesis: Comment', *American Economic Review*, 73(4), 824-7.

Camerer, C. and R.H. Thaler (1995), 'Ultimatums, dictators and manners', *Journal of Economic Perspectives*, 9(2), 209-19.

Clarkson, G.P.E. (1963), *The Theory of Consumer Demand: A Critical Appraisal*, Englewood Cliffs: Prentice-Hall.

Conlisk, J. (1996), 'Why bounded rationality?', *Journal of Economic Literature*, 34(2), 669-700.

Cosmides, L. and J. Tooby (1994), 'Better than rational: Evolutionary psychology and the invisible hand', *American Economic Association Papers and Proceedings*, 84(2), 327-32.

Council of Economic Advisers (1989), *Economic Report of the President*, Washington, DC: US Government Printing Office.

Cox, J.C. and S. Epstein (1989), 'Preference reversals without the independence axiom', *American Economic Review*, 79(3), 408-26.

Cusack, Bob (2003), 'GOP pushes for regulatory reform', *The Hill*, July 8, p. 11.

Davis, N.A. (1993) 'Contemporary deontology', in Peter Singer (ed.), *A Companion to Ethics*, Cambridge, MA: Blackwell Publishers, Ltd., pp. 205-18.

Demsetz, H. (1996), 'The primacy of economics: An explanation of the comparative success of economics in the social sciences', *Economic Inquiry*, 35(1), 1-11.

DePalma, A., G.M. Myers and Y.Y. Papageorgiou (1994), 'Rational choice under an imperfect ability to choose', *American Economic Review*, 84(3), 419-40.

Dowell, R.S., R.S. Goldfarb and W.B. Griffith (1998), 'Economic man as a moral individual', *Economic Inquiry*, 36(4), 645-53.

Duffie, D. and H. Sonnenschein (1989), 'Arrow and general equilibrium theory', *Journal of Economic Literature*, 27(2), 565-98.

Dworkin, Gerald (1995), 'Autonomy', in Robert E. Goodin and Philip Pettit (eds), *A Companion to Contemporary Political Philosophy*, Cambridge, MA: Blackwell Publishers, Ltd., pp. 359-65.

Dworkin, Ronald (1978), *Taking Rights Seriously*, Cambridge, MA: Harvard University Press.

Dworkin, Ronald (1985), *A Matter of Principle*, Cambridge, MA: Harvard University Press.

Dworkin, Ronald (1986), *Law's Empire*, Cambridge, MA: The Belknap Press of Harvard University Press.

Dworkin, R. (1991), 'Foundations of liberal equality', in *Tanner Lectures on Human Values*, Salt Lake City: University of Utah Press.

Ekelund, R.B., E.G. Furubotn and W.P. Gramm (1972), *The Evolution of Modern Demand Theory*, Lexington, MA: D.C. Heath and Company.

Elster, J. (1989), 'Social norms and economic theory', *Journal of Economic Perspectives*, 3(4), 99-117.

Epstein, R. (1973), 'A theory of strict liability', *Journal of Legal Studies*, 2, 151-204.

Epstein, R. (1992), 'Property rights and environmental protection', *Cato Policy Report*, 14.

Etzioni, Amitai (2001), *The Monochrome Society*, Princeton, NJ: Princeton University Press.

Farber, Daniel A. and Suzanna Sherry (2002), *Desperately Seeking Certainty: The Misguided Quest for Constitutional Foundations,* Chicago and London: The University of Chicago Press.

Fehr, E. and S. Gächter (2000), 'Fairness and retaliation: The economics of reciprocity', *Journal of Economic Perspectives*, 14(3), 159-81.

Fields, Gary (2001), 'White House won't fight minority set-aside policy', *Wall Street Journal*, August 13, p. A14.

Foster, J. (2000), 'Is there a role for transaction cost economics if we view firms as complex adaptive systems?', *Contemporary Economic Policy*, 18(4), 369-85.

Frank, R.H. (1987), 'If *Homo Economicus* could choose his own utility function, would he want one with a conscience?', *American Economic Review*, 77(4), 593-604.

Frank, R.H. (1989), 'If *Homo Economicus* could choose his own utility function, would he want one with a conscience: Reply', *American Economic Review*, 79(3), 594-96.

Frank, R.H. (1996), 'The political economy of preference falsification: Timur Kuran's "Private truths, public lies"', *Journal of Economic Literature*, 34(1), 115-23.

Friedman, David D. (2000), *Law's Order*, Princeton, NJ: Princeton University Press.

Friedman, Milton (1953), *Essays in Positive Economics*, Chicago: University of Chicago Press.

Fuller, Lon L. (1971), *The Morality of Law*, New Haven: Yale University Press.

Furubotn, E.G. (1964), 'Investment alternatives and the supply schedule of the firm', *Southern Economic Journal*, 31(1), 21-37.

Furubotn, E.G. (1965), 'The orthodox production function and the adaptability of capital', *Western Economic Journal*, 3(3), 288-300.

Furubotn, E.G. (1970), 'Long-run analysis and the form of the production function', *Economia Internazionale*, 23(1), 3-35.

Furubotn, E.G. (1971), 'Economic organization and welfare distribution', *The Swedish Journal of Economics*, 73(4), 409-16.

Furubotn, E.G. (1991), 'General equilibrium models, transaction costs, and the concept of efficient allocation in a capitalist economy', *Journal of Institutional and Theoretical Economics*, 147(4), 662-86.

Furubotn, E.G. (1994), *Future Development of the New Institutional Economics: Extension of the Neoclassical Model or New Construct?*, Jena: Max-Planck Institute for Research into Economic Systems.

Furubotn, E.G. (1999), 'Economic efficiency in a world of frictions', *Journal of Law and Economics*, 8, 179-97.

Furubotn, Eirik G. and Rudolf Richter (1991), *The New Institutional Economics*, Tübingen: J.C.B. Mohr.

Furubotn, Eirik G. and Rudolf Richter (1997), *Institutions and Economic Theory: The Contribution of the New Institutional Economics*, Ann Arbor: University of Michigan Press.

Garrison, R.W. (1985), 'Predictable behavior: Comment', *American Economic Review*, 75(3), 576-78.

Gauthier, David (1986), *Morals by Agreement*, Oxford: Oxford University Press.

Gewirth, A. (1978), *Reason and Morality*, Chicago: University of Chicago Press.

Gewirth, A. (1982), *Human Rights: Essays on Justification and Application*, Chicago: University of Chicago Press.

Gerwith, David (1986), *Morals by Agreement*, Oxford: Oxford University Press.

Goodin, R.E. (1993), 'Utility and the good', in Peter Singer (ed.), *A Companion to Ethics*, Cambridge, MA: Blackwell Publishers, Ltd., pp. 241-8.

Gort, M. and R. Boddy (1965), 'Vintage effects and the time path of investment in production relations', mimeo, Conference on Research on Income and Wealth, National Bureau of Economic Research, New York.

Graaff, J. de V. (1957), *Theoretical Welfare Economics*, Cambridge: Cambridge University Press.

Grossman, G. and E. Helpman (1994), 'Protection for sale', *American Economic Review*, 84(4), 833-50.

Haavelmo, T. (1997), 'Econometrics and the welfare state', *American Economic Review*, 87(6), 13-5.

Hahn, Frank (1982), 'On some difficulties of the utilitarian economist', in A. Sen and B. Williams (eds), *Utilitarianism and Beyond*, Cambridge: Cambridge University Press, pp. 187-98.

Hahn, R.W. (1998), 'Government analysis of the benefits and costs of regulation', *Journal of Economic Perspectives*, 12(4), 201-10.

Hampton, Jean (1995), 'Contract and consent', in Robert E. Goodin and Philip Pettit (eds), *A Companion to Contemporary Political Philosophy*, Cambridge, MA: Blackwell Publishers, Ltd., pp. 379-93.

Harbough, W.T. and K. Krause (2000), 'Children's altruism in public good and dictator experiments', *Economic Inquiry*, 38(1), 95-109.

Harrington, J.E., Jr. (1989), 'If *Homo Economicus* could choose his own utility function, would he want one with a conscience?: Comment', *American Economic Review*, 79(3), 588-93.

Hart, H.L.A. (1995), 'Are there any natural rights?', in Jeremy Waldron (ed.) (1995), *Theories of Rights*, New York: Oxford University Press, pp. 77-90.

Hatch, O. (Senate) (1981), *Report to Accompany Senate Joint Resolution 58, Balanced Budget-Tax Limitation Amendment*, Washington, DC: US Government Printing Office.

Hausman, D.M. and M.S. McPherson (1993), 'Taking ethics seriously: Economics and contemporary moral philosophy', *Journal of Economic Literature*, 31(2), 671-731.

Hausman, D.M. and M.S. McPherson (1996), *Economic Analysis and Moral Philosophy*, Cambridge: Cambridge University Press.

Hayek, Friedrich A. (1988), *The Fatal Conceit: The Errors of Socialism*, Chicago: University of Chicago Press.

Heiner, R.A. (1983), 'The origin of predictable behavior', *American Economic Review*, 73(4), 560-95.

Heiner, R.A. (1985a), 'Origin of predictable behavior: Further modeling and applications', *American Economic Association Papers and Proceedings*, 75(2), 391-96.

Heiner, R.A. (1985b), 'Predictable behavior: Reply', *American Economic Review*, 75(3), 579-85.

Henrich, J. (2000), 'Does culture matter in economic behavior? Ultimatum game bargaining among the machiguena of the Peruvian Amazon', *American Economic Review*, 90(4), 973-9.

Higginbotham, F.M. and K. Bergin (2003), 'The court has granted wide deference to colleges', *The Chronicle of Higher Education*, March 28.

Hume, David (1739), *A Treatise on Human Nature*, London: Penguin Books (1985).

Hunter, James Davison (2000), *The Death of Character*, New York: Basic Books.

Kaen, F.R. and R.E. Rosenman (1986), 'Predictable behavior in financial markets: Some evidence in support of Heiner's hypothesis', *American Economic Review*, 76(1), 212-20.

Kahneman, D. (2003), 'A psychological perspective on economics', *American Economic Association Papers and Proceedings*, 93(2), 162-8.

Kant, I. (1785), *Fundamental Principles of the Metaphysic of Morals*, translated by T.K. Abbot (1988), New York: Prometheus Books.

Kersting, W. (1992), 'Politics, freedom, and order: Kant's political philosophy', in Paul Guyer (ed.), *The Cambridge Companion to Kant*, Cambridge, MA: Cambridge University Press.

Khalil, E.L. (2002), 'Is Adam Smith a liberal?', Journal of Institutional and Theoretical Economics, 158(4), 664-94.

King, Neil, Jr. (2002), 'U.S. companies cry foul at procedure for granting exemptions to steel tariffs', The Wall Street Journal, March 19, p. A2.

Klamer, A. (1989), 'A conversation with Amartya Sen', Journal of Economic Perspectives, 3(1), 135-50.

Knox, T.M. (1999), 'The volunteer's folly and socio-economic man: Some thoughts on altruism, rationality, and community', The Journal of Socio-economics, 28(4), 475-92.

Krause, Sharon R. (2002), Liberalism with Honor, Cambridge, MA: Harvard University Press.

Kumins, Lawrence C. (1995), 'West coast oil exports', CRS Report to Congress, July 31, pp. 1-8.

Kuran, Timur (1991), 'Cognitive limitations and preference evolution', Journal of Institutional and Theoretical Economics, 147(2), 241-73.

Kymlicka, W. (1993), 'The social contract tradition', in Peter Singer (ed.), A Companion to Ethics, Cambridge, MA: Blackwell Publishers, Ltd., pp. 186-96.

Lee, Christopher (2003), '2002 Federal Register is longest ever', Washington Post, July 8, p. A15.

Leontief, W. (1971), 'Theoretical assumptions and nonobserved facts', American Economic Review, 61(1), 74-81.

Lewin, S.B. (1996), 'Economics and psychology: Lessons for our own day from the early twentieth century', Journal of Economic Literature, 34(3), 1293-323.

Lipsey, R. and K. Lancaster (1956), 'The general theory of second best', Review of Economic Studies, 24(63), 11-32.

Lyons, David (1982), 'Utility and rights', in Jeremy Waldron (ed.) (1995), Theories of Rights, New York: Oxford University Press, pp. 110-36.

Macedo, Stephen (1995), 'Toleration and fundamentalism', in Robert E. Goodin and Philip Pettit (eds), A Companion to Contemporary Political Philosophy, Cambridge, MA: Blackwell Publishers, Ltd. pp. 622-8.

MacDonald, Margaret (1947-1948), 'Natural Rights', in Jeremy Waldron (ed.) (1995), Theories of Rights, New York: Oxford University Press, pp. 21-40.

Mayer, Thomas (1993), Truth versus Precision in Economics, Aldershot, UK and Brookfield, US: Edward Elgar.

Melitz, J. (1965), 'Friedman and Machlup on the significance of testing economic assumptions', Journal of Political Economy, 73(1), 37-60.

Mercuro, Nicholas and Steven G. Medema (1997), *Economics and the Law: From Posner to Post-Modernism*, Princeton, NJ: Princeton University Press.

Mill, John Stuart (1838), 'Bentham', reprinted in Gertrude Himmelfarb (ed.) (1990), *John Stuart Mill, Essays on Politics and Culture*, New York: Peter Smith Publishing, Inc..

Mill, John Stuart (1859), *On Liberty*, reprinted in Stefan Collini (ed.) (2000), *Cambridge Texts in the History of Political Thought*, Cambridge: Cambridge University Press.

Miller, G.J. (1997), 'The impact of economics on contemporary political science', *Journal of Economic Literataure*, 35(3), 1173-204.

Mitra, D. (1999), 'Endogenous lobby formation and endogenous protection: A long-run model of trade policy determination', *American Economic Review*, 89(5), 1116-34.

Muller, Jerry Z. (1993), *Adam Smith in His Time and Ours: Designing the Decent Society*, Princeton, NJ: Princeton University Press.

Murray, Shailagh and Neil King, Jr. (2003), 'Congress faces duel in export-tax repeal', *The Wall Street Journal*, July 16, p. A4.

Nagel, E. (1963), 'Assumptions in economic theory', *American Economic Association Papers and Proceedings*, 53(2), 211-19.

Nelson, J.A. (1995), 'Feminism and economics', *Journal of Economic Perspectives*, 9(2), 131-48.

North, D.C. (1994), 'Economic performance through time', *American Economic Review*, 84(3), 359-68.

Novshek, W. and H. Sonnenschein (1987), 'General equilibrium with free entry: A synthetic approach to the theory of perfect competition', *Journal of Economic Literature*, 25(3), 1281-306.

Nozick, Robert (1974), *Anarchy, State and Utopia*, New York: Basic Books.

Office of Management and Budget (2001), *Analytical Perspectives*, Budget of the United States Government, Fiscal Year 2002, Washington, DC: US Government Printing Office.

Office of Management and Budget (2001), *A Citizen's Guide to the Federal Budget*, Budget of the United States Government, Fiscal Year 2002, Washington, DC: US Government Printing Office.

Office of Management and Budget (2003), *Analytical Perspectives*, Budget of the United States Government, Fiscal Year 2004, Washington, DC: US Government Printing Office.

Office of Management and Budget (2003), *Budget*, Budget of the United States Government, Fiscal Year 2004, Washington, DC: US Government Printing Office.

Office of Management and Budget (2003), *Historical Tables*, Budget of the United States Government, Fiscal Year 2004, Washington, DC: US Government Printing Office.

O'Neill, O. (1993), 'Kantian ethics', in Peter Singer (ed.), *A Companion to Ethics*, Cambridge, MA: Blackwell Publishers, Ltd., pp. 175-85.

Ornstein, Norman J., Thomas E. Mann and Michael I. Malbin (2000), *Vital Statistics in Congress, 1999-2000*, Washington, DC: The AEI Press.

Ostrom, E. (2000), 'Collective action and the evolution of social norms', *Journal of Economic Perspectives*, 14(3), 137-58.

Pareto, V. (1896), 'Cours d'economie politique', cited in Senator Orrin Hatch (1981), *Report to Accompany Senate Joint Resolution 58, Balanced Budget-Tax Limitation Amendment*, Washington, DC: United States Government Printing Office.

Parks, A. Lee, Jr. (2003), 'Racial diversity's effect on education is a myth', *The Chronicle of Higher Education*, March 28.

Paton, H.J. (1964), *Immanuel Kant Groundwork of the Metaphysic of Morals*, New York: Harper Torchbooks.

Pettit, P. (1993), 'Consequentialism', in Peter Singer (ed.), *A Companion to Ethics*, Cambridge, MA: Blackwell Publishers, Ltd., pp. 230-40.

Phillips, Michael M. and Laura Heinauer (2001), 'Exporters rush to Ex-Im Bank's defense, *The Wall Street Journal*, March 7, p. A2.

Pingle, M. (1992), 'Costly optimization: An experiment', *Journal of Economic Behavior and Organization*, 17(1), 3-30.

Pollak, R.A. (1985), 'A transaction cost approach to families and households', *Journal of Economic Literature*, 13(2), 581-608.

Posner, Richard A. (1986), *Economic Analysis of Law*, Boston and Toronto: Little, Brown and Company.

Quinton, A. (1995), 'Conservatism', in Robert E. Goodin and Philip Pettit (eds), *A Companion to Contemporary Political Philosophy*, Cambridge, MA: Blackwell Publishers, Ltd., pp. 244-68.

Rabin, M. and R.H. Thaler (2001), 'Risk aversion', *Journal of Economic Perspectives*, 15(1), 219-32.

Rachels, James (1993), 'Subjectivism', in Peter Singer (ed.), *A Companion to Ethics*, Cambridge, MA: Blackwell Publishers, Ltd., pp. 432-41.

Rawls, John (1971), *A Theory of Justice*, Cambridge, MA: The Belknap Press of Harvard University Press.

Rawls, John (1989), 'Themes in Kant's moral philosophy', in Samuel Freeman (ed.) (1999), *John Rawls: Collected Papers*, Cambridge, MA: Harvard University Press, pp. 497-528.

Robinson, Joan (1962), *Economic Philosophy*, London: C.A. Watts & Co.

Robson, A. J. (2001), 'The biological basis of economic behavior', *Journal of Economic Literature*, 39(1), 11-33.

Roth, T.P. (1972), 'The subjective production function: An approach to its determination', *The Engineering Economist*, 17(4), 249-59.

Roth, T.P. (1974), 'The demand for a single variable productive service and the adaptability of capital', *Artha Vijnana*, 15(4), 421-31.

Roth, T.P. (1977), 'Imperfect knowledge and the problem of choice among alternative production techniques', *The Engineering Economist*, 22(4), 277-97.

Roth, T.P. (1979), 'Empirical cost curves and the production-theoretic short-run: A reconciliation', *Quarterly Review of Economics and Business*, 19(3), 35-47.

Roth, Timothy (1998), *The Present State of Consumer Theory: The Implications for Social Welfare Theory*, Lanham, MD, New York and Oxford: University Press of America.

Roth, Timothy (1999), *Ethics, Economics and Freedom: The Failure of Consequentialist Social Welfare Theory*, Aldershot, UK and Brookfield US: Ashgate.

Roth, T.P. (2002), *The Ethics and the Economics of Minimalist Government*, Cheltenham, UK and Northampton, MA: Edward Elgar.

Russell, T. and R. Thaler (1985), 'The relevance of quasi-rationality in competitive markets', *American Economic Review*, 75(5), 1071-82.

Ryan, A. (1995), 'Liberalism', in Robert E. Goodin and Philip Pettit (eds), *A Companion to Contemporary Political Philosophy*, Cambridge, MA: Blackwell Publishers, Ltd., pp. 291-311.

Salanié, Bernard (2000), *The Microeconomics of Market Failure*, Cambridge, MA and London: The MIT Press.

Sandel, Michael J. (1996), *Democracy's Discontent: America in Search of a Public Philosophy*, Cambridge, MA: The Belknap Press of Harvard University Press.

Sandmo, A. (1990), 'Buchanan on political economy: A review article', *Journal of Economic Literature*, 28(1), 50-65.

Scruton, Roger (1982), *Kant*, Oxford: Oxford University Press.

Scruton, Roger (1994), *Modern Philosophy: An Introduction and Survey*, New York: Penguin Books.

Scruton, Roger (1996), *An Intelligent Person's Guide to Philosophy*, New York: Penguin Books.

Scruton, Roger (2002), *The Meaning of Conservatism*, South Bend, IN: St. Augustine's Press.

Sen, Amartya (1992), *Inequality Reexamined*, Cambridge, MA: Harvard University Press.

Sen, A. (1995), 'Rationality and social choice', *American Economic Review*, 85(1), 1-24.

Simon, Herbert A. (1992), 'Introductory comment', in Massimo Egide, Robin Marris and Ricardo Viale (eds), *Economics, Bounded Rationality and the Cognitive Revolution*, Aldershot, UK and Brookfield, US: Edward Elgar, pp. 3-7.

Simon, Herbert A. (1996), *The Sciences of the Artificial*, Third Edition, Cambridge, MA: The MIT Press.

Skinner, Q. (1991), 'The paradox of political liberty', in D. Miller (ed.), *Liberty*, Oxford University Press, pp. 183-205.

Slesnick, D. (1998), 'Empirical approaches to the measurement of welfare', *Journal of Economic Literature*, 36(4), 2108-65.

Smith, Adam (1759), *The Theory of Moral Sentiments*, reprinted in D.D. Raphael and A.L. Macfie (eds) (1976), The Glasgow Edition of *The Works and Correspondence of Adam Smith*, Oxford: Oxford University Press.

Smith, Adam (1776), *An Inquiry into the Nature and Causes of the Wealth of Nations*, reprinted in W.B. Todd (ed.) (1976), The Glasgow Edition of *The Works and Correspondence of Adam Smith*, vol. II, Oxford: Oxford University Press.

Smith, V. (1985), 'Experimental economics: Reply', *American Economic Review*, 75(1), 265-72.

Smith, V. (1989), 'Theory, experiment and economics', *Journal of Economic Perspectives*, 3(1), 115-69.

Smith, V. (2003), 'Constructivist and ecological rationality in economics', *American Economic Review*, 93(3), 465-508.

Snyder, Jim (2003), 'We think this is just outrageous', *The Hill*, July 8, p. 13.

Stigler, George (1987), *The Theory of Price*, New York: Macmillan.

Stigler, G. and G.S. Becker (1977), 'De qustibus non est disputandum', *American Economic Review*, 67(2), 76-90.

Stiglitz, Joseph (1994), *Whither Socialism*, Cambridge, MA: MIT Press.

Sugden, R. (1993), 'Welfare, resources and capabilities: A review of *Inequality Reexamined* by Amartya Sen', *Journal of Economic Literature*, 31(4), 1947-62.

Supreme Court of the United States, *Bowers v. Hardwick*, 478 U.S. (1986).

Supreme Court of the United States, *Lawrence et al. v. Texas*, 539 U.S. (2003).

Supreme Court of the United States, *Regents of the University of California v. Bakke*, 348 US (1978).

Tappan, Mark B. and Lyn Mikel Brown (1989), 'Stories told and lessons learned: Toward a narrative approach to moral development and moral education', *Harvard Education Review*, 59(2).

Tebbit, Mark (2000), *Philosophy of Law*, London: Routledge.

Ten, C.L. (1995), 'Constitutionalism and the rule of law', in Robert E. Goodin and Philip Pettit (eds), *A Companion to Contemporary Political Philosophy*, Cambridge, MA: Blackwell Publishers Ltd., pp. 394-403.

Thaler, R.H. (2000), 'From *homo economicus* to *homo sapiens*', *Journal of Economic Perspectives*, 14(1), 133-41.

Tversky, A. and R.H. Thaler (1990), 'Preference reversals', *Journal of Economic Perspectives*, 4(2), 201-11.

US Congress Joint Economic Committee (1979), *The 1979 Joint Economic Report*, Washington, DC: US Government Printing Office.

Waldron, J. (1987), 'Theoretical foundations of liberalism', *Philosophical Quarterly*, 37, 122-50.

Waldron, J. (1995a), 'Introduction', in Jeremy Waldron (ed.) (1995), *Theories of Rights*, Oxford: Oxford University Press, pp. 1-20.

Waldron, J. (1995b), 'Rights', in Robert E. Goodin and Philip Pettit (eds), *A Companion to Contemporary Political Philosophy*, Cambridge, MA: Blackwell Publishers, Ltd., pp. 575-85.

Weingast, B.R. (1991), 'The political institutions of representativegovernment: Legislatures', in Eirik G. Furubotn and Rudolf Richter (eds), *The New Institutional Economics*, Tübingen: J.C.B. Mohr (Paul Siebeck).

Wilde, K.D., A.D. LeBaron and D. Israelsen (1985), 'Knowledge, uncertainty and behavior', *American Economic Association Papers and Proceedings*, 75(2), 403-08.

Williamson, Oliver E. (1985), *The Economic Institutions of Capitalism*, New York: The Free Press.

Wolfe, Alan (1998), *One Nation After All: What Middle-Class Americans Really Think About God, Country, Family, Racism, Welfare, Immigration, Homosexuality, Work, the Right, the Left, and Each Other*, New York: Viking Penguin.

Wolfe, Alan (2001), *Moral Freedom*, New York: W.W. Norton & Company.

Wong, David (1993), 'Relativism', in Peter Singer (ed.), *A Companion to Ethics*, Cambridge, MA: Blackwell Publishers, Ltd., pp. 442-50.

Wong, Stanley (1973), 'The "F-twist" and the methodology of Paul Samuelson', *American Economic Review*, 63(3), 312-25.

Wood, Peter (2003), *Diversity: The Invention of a Concept*, San Francisco: Encounter Books.

Index